Daniel Bedinger Lucas

The wreath of Eglantine, and other poems

Daniel Bedinger Lucas

The wreath of Eglantine, and other poems

ISBN/EAN: 9783741195976

Manufactured in Europe, USA, Canada, Australia, Japa

Cover: Foto ©Andreas Hilbeck / pixelio.de

Manufactured and distributed by brebook publishing software (www.brebook.com)

Daniel Bedinger Lucas

The wreath of Eglantine, and other poems

THE Wreath of Eglantine,

AND

OTHER POEMS:

Edited and in Part Composed

BY

DANIEL BEDINGER LUCAS.

BALTIMORE:
KELLY, PIET & COMPANY.
1869.

Entered according to Act of Congress, in the year 1868, by

KELLY, PIET & CO.,

In the Clerk's Office of the District Court for the District of Maryland.

KELLY, PIET & CO., PRINTERS.

PREFACE.

SUCH of the pastoral pieces arranged under the title of "THE WREATH OF EGLANTINE" as have been published heretofore, were contributed by the authoress to various Southern journals over the *nomme de plume* of "EGLANTINE."

Of the three stages of poetic life, undoubtedly the first is the *disposition to write verse;* there is then achieved a knowledge of *what poetry is*, before the third and final epoch of power and production. It seems to me, in comparing the earlier and later pieces of "EGLANTINE," that she had attained to a knowledge of what constitutes Poetry, as distinguished from the mere spontaneous and uncultivated outflow of poetic emotion, and that, at her death, on the threshold of her twenty-seventh year, she was treading closely upon that enchanted domain to breathe whose atmosphere is inspiration indeed, and where all things of beauty and harmony supply the ambrosia which nourishes the soul of the genuine Poet.

But whether she would have attained the power of the Poet or not, "EGLANTINE" was endowed, as all who knew her will testify, with his rare susceptibility to the charms of Nature. Flowers were to her companions and interpreters; with them she conversed, and seemed almost in them to renew her own being; her fancy could recall the exact shades of coloring, the dentations and involutes of almost every wild-flower which adorns her own beautiful, native Shenandoah Valley; with a pencil she would sketch, or with her scissors cut any one of them at will, until they were reproduced, apparently in the minute detail and exquisite grace of Nature herself.

The fidelity of her description of rural scenes on the banks of the Shenandoah, some of which the artist has illustrated, will be recognized by those who were lately her fellow-citizens of the Virginia Valley; and beyond these the readers of this volume are scarcely expected widely to extend.

PREFACE.

It is a beautiful thought that the Flora of the region where sleep our ancestors is in fact *related* to us; that a portion of the bodies from which our own are descended, lives also in the plants which surround us; that we ourselves shall survive in them; that Flowers are the Resurrection, and Nature the Immortality of the body!

To all whom God has made susceptible to this and similar thoughts, "EGLANTINE" will speak a language, simple though it be, yet fresh, fragrant, and earnestly pure; and to these kindred spirits her "Wreath" is offered by

THE EDITOR.

CONTENTS.

WREATH OF EGLANTINE:

	PAGE.
Morning Dawn	11
Rural Afternoon	12
Early Twilight	14
Summer Night	17
The Stars	19
Autumn Scene	21
The Cottage by the Mill	23
The Blue Forget-Me-Not	25
The Grape-Vine Swing	27
Recollections of Erie	29
Indian Summer	31
A Night Scene	34
The Ruin	35
Meeting of the Shenandoah and Potomac	38
Lines to a Cedar of Lebanon	41
October Musings	43

PATRIOTIC AND NATIONAL POEMS:

The Land Where we Were Dreaming	63
The Battle of Ball's Bluff	67
My Heart is in the Mountains	69
Song of the South	70

CONTENTS.

	PAGE.
JEFFERSON DAVIS	72
ODE RECITED AT THE CONSECRATION OF THE STONEWALL CEMETERY	73
THE VIRGINIANS SIT AND WEEP	79

TINTOGRAPHIC MELODIES:

CALIDIA	83
NIVEAN	90
LORA LOGIE	98
UNDERNEATH THE FULLNESS	100
TO MISS NANNIE B******	101
EGLANTINE	102
THE FLOWERS WE CALL FLORA	105
THE PICTURE	105
CORINNE	106
LUCILE	108
'TWAS IN THE GENTLE TWILIGHT SEASON	110
MARY	111
O, SWEET AT MORNING'S DEWY DAWN	112
MY THOUGHT GROWS HAZY WITH THE SEASON'S TOUCH	113
O, LORA, AS THE EARTH PURSUES	114
A SERENADE	115
THE WIND CHIMED LOW	116
THE SOLITARY HORSEMAN	117
THERE ARE PRECIOUS CARGOES STRANDED	119
OUT ON THE SEASHORE	120

SAINT AGNES OF GUIENNE 123

MORNING DAWN.

HOW sweet the hour, how fair the scene, as o'er
  The dreamy mountain-top's delicious blue,
  The first faint streakings of the pearly dawn,
  And growing brightness of the shifting clouds,
Forewarn the far-off glittering Star of Morn—
Of Day's approach! How swiftly flee the shades
Of Night from o'er the deep ravines, and vales
Secluded 'mid the hills, and every still
Recess, o'erhung by dark'ning forest boughs!

Where fields of matted clover, tangled with
A thousand webs of shining pearls, breathe out
Fresh perfume on the air, hums the wild bee
His morning hymn. Along the meadow-path,
And by the brook, where greener grows the grass,
The tufted blossoms lift their yellow crests
To catch the dew-drop shaken from the blade.

Soft-flooding, steals the rosy light along
The silver sky, dispelling fog and vapor,
Till at last the golden-skirted clouds
Shine with the Sun's reflected radiance!

Lo! brightly breaks the blazing light of day,
And the new-risen Orb smiles on the face
Of Nature; while the notes of many birds,
In mingling chorus, greet him far and near!

A RURAL AFTERNOON.

O HERE 'tis sweet to stray, afar from men,
  Lost in the shadows of this leafy glen!
Here, 'mid the velvet moss and lace-like fern,
Many a blossom lifts its dewy urn;
The snow-white fringe-tree droops in soft perfume,
And the wild honey-suckles, bell-like, bloom;
And oft at eve, among these bowers of green,
The red-bird, sweet ventriloquist, is seen,
Whose pensive notes still seem to float from far,
Like music wafted from the vesper star.

A RURAL AFTERNOON.

The wild bee stays his flight the brook to drink,
Or sips the blue-bell nodding on the brink.
While turkey-grape, and many a native vine,
Along the banks their tangled garlands twine;
And yonder, dripping down the mountain side,
Trickles the parent fountain's foaming tide—
Purest of waters is that rock-fed spring!
Freshest of flowers those that round it cling!
The mountain rills, and wood-nursed flowers for me,
That flow, and bloom, where pathless winds blow free!
Let others love the city's noise and glare—
Give me the breezy height, the forest air!
The peacefulness of such calm scenes calls back
The spirit restless on life's hurried track
Of vanity and folly, grief and pain,
To quaff at Nature's fresh'ning founts again;
And thus I turn, in pensive silence now,
To yonder mountain's blue and tranquil brow,
As erst, still changeless, lovely and serene—
Musing on all that is—on all that might have been!
The golden dawn of health has passed away,
And gone the young delights of April's day,
When joy was rapture, tears a sudden shower
That only brightened the succeeding hour;
But higher thoughts, and holier hopes are mine,
And like the smile of twilight's soft decline,

As from the mountain side slow sinks the sun,
My days, in peaceful calm, glide smoothly on;
And when, ere long, my form in dust is laid,
Let me but sleep beneath the Blue-Ridge shade,
While o'er my head its murmuring winds shall sweep,
And dewdrop-bending blossoms gently weep!

EARLY TWILIGHT.

WAN as the snow-white thorn, hangs the thin New-moon,
  Her slender crescent o'er the Eve-star's eye!
And wafted lightly on the wild, sweet breath
Of rose-lipped Evening, thro' the sapphire deep,
Clouds, in the sultry-purple West, hang low—
Beautiful waifs of air, floating their locks
Of gold, athwart the breast of the still sky!
The zephyrs brush away the falling tears
That gather bright upon the leafy boughs,
And shadowy grass, dusk in the faint star-light.
The garden gates are shut; and shut the violet's eye,
And crimson-shaded tulip's glowing lips;
The blue and melancholy hyacinth

EARLY TWILIGHT.

Hangs heavy in the twilight's deep'ning gloom,
Struck by Apollo's western-glancing quoit;
The pensive snow-drops droop their green-tipped cups,
And silver-bells are nestled 'mong the deep
Green leaves, hoarding their balmy breath within,
Like timid breasts that tremble to disclose
The hidden sweetness of their own pure thoughts—
Would that their hearts were more enduring!

      Hark!
A sweet sound breaks upon the ear close by;
It is the red-bird warbling on the rose-bush
Now his nightly lay, singing as tho'
He would pour out his very soul in one
Wild gush of melody! Sweet messenger
Of hope, whence comest thou? And wherefore is
Thy song so joyous? Art thou cheering
Thy mate upon her nest near by? Or art
Thou vocal only for it is thy nature,
And sing'st thou know'st nor carest why? Sing on!
Gay bird, thy silvery voice disturbeth not
The scene, whose melting loveliness hath waked
Thy song! 'Tis but appropriate expression,
And thou dost speak sweet Nature's inmost thought!

The Birds! the bright-eyed Birds! Their carols bring
To mind our guileless years—the mild May-day

EARLY TWILIGHT.

When we went strolling o'er the sunny fields,
Rejoicing on our way, and gathering
The nodding bells along the mossy ledge,
Or paused beside the shady forest path
To pluck the early-fading flowers, while squirrels
Playful sprang from bough to arching bough
Above our heads, or ran along the rails.

These birds do seem to breathe a freer air,
And their wild music echoes less of sin
And sorrow—more of bliss—than aught below:
And when the pure and lovely sink in death,
Like yon brief star, fast fading in the West—
When the green turf puts on its vernal freshness,
And the boughs burst forth in bud and bloom—
The Birds, like winged seraphs, hover o'er
Their gentle heads, and sing of hope and heaven!

SUMMER NIGHT.

THE night is lovelier than the day!
   Round-rising o'er the distant trees,
Floats the fair moon, with cloudless ray,
   And faintly blows the trembling breeze:
Lo! soft the Shenandoah's flow
   Upon the South-wind's lips is borne,
While down its current, gliding slow,
   Lonely the boatman winds his horn.

SUMMER NIGHT.

Watchful, above in sleepless gleam,
    O'er the dark hills in pale array,
Scarce seen beneath the full moon's beam,
    The small stars spot the heaven's clear gray:
With folded arms the mountains stand,
    In silence, o'er the river's brim,
While willows, where they shade the sand,
    Nod to their image in the stream.

Beneath, the frogs in chorus sing;
    The glimmering glow-worm glides between,
And rising slow, on flashing wing,
    The fire-fly sparkles o'er the scene:
The fox peers from the covered brake,
    And noiselessly descends the steep;
Out from the thicket steals the snake,
    And bright-eyed lizards pertly creep.

Issuing forth in quest of food,
    From hollow trunk or knarled root,
In the deep silence of the wood,
    The horned owl prolongs his hoot;
Blinded no more by day's broad glare,
    The clinging bat his culvert leaves,
And circling through the soundless air,
    Darts swiftly round the dusky eaves.

Where the dark jasmin droops below,
   Dropping full many a spotless cup,
Soft o'er the white bloom's scattered snow,
   The odorous breath of buds floats up:
Now loosely hanging o'er the blind,
   The ivy taps upon the pane,
And, restless, rustles in the wind—
   A pause—and all is still again.

But calmly on, and lovely still,
   Yon pale orb floats from star to star,
And pensive cries the whippoorwill,
   And barks the watch-dog from afar:
Musing, with fresh emotions fraught,
   I own thy soul-subduing power,
Sacred to sleep and silent thought,
   O! sweet and melancholy hour!

THE STARS.

THE Night is here—the deep, the dark, still Night,
  With stars on stars, a countless multitude!
The glittering Wain its steadfast course pursues;
Proud Sirius blazes from afar; the sister

THE STARS.

Virgins shine with soft and chasten'd light;
And sinking in the south, the Warrior waves
His sword of fire, and girts his golden belt!
Magnificent Orion! Who that e'er
Beheld thy bright meridian radiance can
Forget thy form's surpassing splendor, 'mid
The host that fills the chambers of the South,
Whose gliding steps, most eloquently mute,
Keep time to nature's laws?
      Yet have ye voices
O, ye stars! and tongues of flame, that, heard
Not by the ear, can pierce the secret soul,
And kindle sympathy akin to you,
Too deep for utterance! Ambition's breast
Hath been laid bare to you, whose restless thoughts
Their sleepless vigils keep by your lone lamps:
Pride lays aside her mask to you alone;
Youth's burning aspirations and its hopes,
By you are kindled; or age yields to you
Its dream, whose bright fulfillment, looked for now
No longer, was the end and goal of life's
Most cherished purposes; for few or none
Accomplish all they've planned, or even much
They might have done in life's allotted years;
But failing in their aim, yet not in vain
The high resolves, the noble impulses

That fire and renovate the source of all
Our thought; they quicken into being hopes,
And feelings which remain when that which first
Awoke them fails.
                These are the things of which
The stars bear record; nor of these alone;
Beneath their soft, congenial ray, young Love
First breathes his warm, impassioned soul;
Or fortunate or idle, vain or crowned,
The earth hath ne'er a second strain like his!

AUTUMN SCENE.

THE tranquil autumn days are here again.
   The lazy herds are lowing in the lane,
And idle insects flutter in the air
Of purple-tinted groves and pastures fair:
The orchards now their mellow fruitage yield,
The ripened corn is gathered in the field,
As slowly winding o'er the peaceful plain
The cheerful farmer drives his lumb'ring wain.

AUTUMN SCENE.

The golden rod is blooming in the wood;
And soft amid its pensive lonelihood,
While ever and anon the ripe nuts fall,
Is heard the turtle-dove's sweet mournful call,
The jay's shrill scream, the crow's complaining croak,
And far away the ax's ringing stroke.

Yellow and amber, pink, purple and red,
Rustles the leafy canopy o'er head;
Beneath, the asters, glistening in the dew,
A flowery carpet weave of wavy blue,
While blending with the pale pine's feathery green,
The cedar's azure-tinted crest is seen.

The maple, with its golden-orange glow,
Bends softly o'er the river's shining flow;
The spreading sycamore extends beside,
Dropping its long, bare branches o'er the tide;
Fast to its twisted roots is moored a skiff;
A rocky path above ascends the cliff;
While round the brink the graceful hemlocks grow—
The alder droops its berried bough below.

But silent now the shore, and lonely all,
As one by one the bright leaves floating fall;
Out o'er the wave appears one faint, sweet star,
Half-timidly, though radiantly fair!

THE COTTAGE BY THE MILL.

The daylight dies upon the distant hill;
But in the balmy West, in mute appeal,
Hovers a lovely cloud of rosy-violet,
Like lingering hope, when all but hope hath set!

THE COTTAGE BY THE MILL.

WHEN the soft shades of twilight are gathering nigh,
And the lone star of evening appears in the sky,
As the voice of the night-wind falls faint on my ear,
I think of the scenes which in childhood were dear;

THE COTTAGE BY THE MILL.

Of the streamlet that flowed thro' the meadow of old,
Where I gathered the butter-cup blossoms of gold,
And the cot where I dwelt at the foot of the hill—
The vine-covered cottage that stood by the mill.

The wild-waving willow whose green boughs bent o'er,
And the clustering lilac that grew by the door,
Where I listened all day, as I played, to the sound
Of the mill with its great wooden wheel going round:
With my fair little sister, who died long ago,
With her light golden hair, and her cheeks like the snow,
As pure as the white rose that climbed o'er the sill
Of the sweet shady cottage that stood by the mill.

Now the meadow is gay with the butter-cup's gold,
The green willow bends to the breeze as of old;
The mill is still standing, the cot is still there,
The rose is still blooming as fragrant and fair;
And the lilac-bush waving dispenses perfume—
But the hand of another now gathers the bloom;
And the face of a stranger looks out from the sill
Of the neat, white-washed cottage that stands by the mill.

THE BLUE FORGET-ME-NOT.

"There is a flower, a lovely flower
  Tinged deep with faith's unchanging hue."—HALLECK.

ONE sweet song, with magic power,
    Thrilled my spirit erè I knew
That my native forest's bower
    Held that lovely gem, the blue
            Forget-me-not.

Still, that flower's blue-eyed blossom,
    Bending o'er the quiet stream,
Whispers to this haunted bosom,
    Brooding o'er a vanished dream—
            Forget-me-not!

Tho' our life's bright vision over,
    Henceforth we roam the world apart—
Tho' love's light be lost forever,
    In the silence of thy heart
            Forget-me-not!

On the brow of dewy even,
    When the vesper-star beams bright,
As the sunset hues of heaven
    Fade and melt into the night—
            Forget-me-not!

THE BLUE FORGET-ME-NOT.

Ling'ring by the lonely river,
   And the darkly-waving wood,
Listing but the wild wind's murmur,
   In thy spirit's solitude
               Forget-me-not!

When the sound of music stealing
   From a spirit sad and lone,
Stirs a chord of deepest feeling,
   And awakes an answering tone,
               Forget-me-not!

When the mournful muse hath spoken
   Of the lost—the early dead—
Loving hearts too lightly broken—
   Bending o'er my lowly head,
               Forget-me-not!

Never with its hues were blended
   Youth and bloom and joyance yet,
Still till life and love be ended,
   Speaks that blossom's deep regret—
               Forget-me-not!

THE GRAPE-VINE SWING.

WHERE the tall oaks threw their spreading shade,
Back and forth in the breeze the wild-grape swayed;
The shaggy trunk, all twisted and old,
Was bent in many a serpent-like fold.

Still lazily swinging to and fro,
Over the rill that sparkled below,
While the birds above were used to sing
Thro' the leafy loops of the grape-vine swing.

From bough to bough, a glossy wreath,
The gay wild blossoms sprang up beneath,
The cowslip pale, and the violet blue,
And the cardinal's plumes of brilliant hue—
But none of these buds that bloomed at its feet,
Had a scent that was half so fresh and sweet
As the green-waving flowers that used to cling
To the graceful folds of the grape-vine swing.

I gathered the ferns around its root,
And moss-cups small, with their tiny fruit,
Painting me pictures of the days to be.
There's a picture now comes back to me—
'Tis a vision fair of a sunny child,
With hands full of buds and blossoms wild.
Alas! for the shadows that dark days fling,
O'er the once sunny face in the grape-vine swing.

RECOLLECTIONS OF ERIE.

FAIR and far away Lake Erie's glassy waters flow;
    Upon its spreading wave soft shines the silver moon;
Its burnished breast reflects the evening sunset's glow,
    Or blue within, the still skies lie at summer noon.

Above, the gray clouds move in measured silence on,
    And cool and soft below, their shadowy shapes are seen,
While o'er the dreamy deep her wild wing waves the swan,
    Seeking her nest among the reeds and rushes green.

Pure is the breeze, whose light lips fan the breathing tide,
    Filling the sail of many a white bark gliding there;
Peaceful the shore whose lovely landscape sleeps beside,
    Save when the rushing rail-car's rumble breaks the air;

Or starting steamboats whistle at the dawn of day,
    From where the distant city's shining spires appear,
Whose winding wreaths of blue smoke rise and float away,
    As its low murmur falls upon the listening ear—

Fast fading with its dreamy domes and dwellings fair—
    Its silver-glittering beach, and gardens gay within,

As those grand piles dissolve—we scarce know how or
    where—
  Whose gorgeous towers and spires at sunset's gates are
    seen.

Nor ken we more of hearts that beat beneath its walls,
  Save that the mortal immortality puts on,
Than of the spirits who perchance inhabit halls
  Beyond the golden portals of the setting sun.

Through years of waste and change, though miles of
    space divide,
  Those far-off waters, cold and clear in bluish light—
Those city spires, those skies imprinting on the tide
  Their dream of solemn rest—still haunt my fancy's
    sight!

INDIAN SUMMER.

THE crimson Sun is slowly sinking in the West;
   The mournful wind is sighing through the vale;
Soft twilight shadows tremble o'er the streamlet's breast,
   And Autumn leaves are lifted by the gale.
Nature smiles in all the wondrous beauty of decay;
   The verdant meads—the woods, with brilliant hue,
Reflecting the rich glory of the dying day—
   Are painted on a field of boundless blue.

The green, sparse grain is peering out from its rich mold,
   Not in the dense luxuriance of May,

Nor waves it in the breeze, with harvest's gleam of gold,
    But every blade, in velvet-green array,
Assumes a yellow tinge, as streams of orange light
    Are pouring gently on the soft, moist clod,
And teaching that the Sun, who paints in glory bright
    The curtained East, stoops to the humblest sod.

The far-off mountain-tops, agleam with rosy light,
    While shadows lie between of softest blue,
Are changing with the day's departing beams: their height
    Now glows in purple splendor; now its hue
Still takes a deeper dye, as gum with maple blends,
    While poplars intertwine their golden boughs;
And many a silver-sparkling streamlet softly wends
    His rimpling pathway where the linden grows.

Beyond the birch, mixed with the oak-leaf's crimson dye,
    The drooping willow, verdant still, is seen;
And o'er each rocky cliff that lifts its head on high
    The lordly pine and laurel-leaf are green:
The barking squirrel stores his hollow tree within
    Shell-barks and dusky walnuts for his hoard,
And burs ajar, disclosing ripe, brown nuts between,
    With rock-oak acorns, full supplies afford.

Round many a rocky brink is hung a scarlet vine,
    Whose tempting clusters dangle in the air,

INDIAN SUMMER.

Where sassafras and grape-vine lovingly entwine,
   And thorny boughs their purple berries wear;
The timid rabbit hides him in the stones beneath,
   And slyly nestles in the withered grass,
Secure, nor hears nor heeds the hound upon the heath,
   Unless my step should scare him as I pass.

The coral berries of the bitter-sweet are ripe,
   That long ago its light-green leaves has shed;
Within the forest's depths the fragile Indian pipe
   Lifts up its waxen stalk, and pale, pure head—
Up-springing in the wildwood's now deserted bowers,
   In pearly clusters from its leafy bed,
The loveliest and last of all cold Autumn's flowers,
   It blooms in lonely beauty round the dead!

As some fair girl doth tremble at her lover's tone,
   Ash and shumac leaves, of blushing dye,
Now quiver as the zephyr claims them for his own,
   And to his soft caresses gently sigh:—
Oh! wild and melancholy-sweet the wind's low noise!
   These fading leaves are spirits fleeting by
Upon the breath of Heaven, and a sweet, sad voice
   Of Nature plains that they should early die!

For beauty born of swift decay is gleaming there;
   Each shining leaf but brightens as it dies,

Like the feverish flush Death's human victims wear,
    Too richly bright for these dim earthly skies;
Alas! ye lovely, soulless things, 'tis not for you
    My fainting spirit mourns, although ephemeral—
Ye are but leaves that Spring will soon or late renew—
    To me the West wind breathes a sadder tale!

A NIGHT SCENE.

THE night is calm and clear, and many a quiet star,
    Is shining in the stilly depths of heaven serene,
While the late-rising moon peers o'er the mount afar,
    And streaks with silver light each branching evergreen.

On yonder hill the white tents stand like drifts of show;
    A hundred canon lie upon its grassy steep,
A hundred fires are blazing in the vale below;
    But not a murmur stirs the war-worn soldier's sleep.

And neither sky-lark's song, nor owlet's cry is heard
    Breaking the hushed stillness of the dream-like air;
Yet stay—there is a sound?—'twas but the ivy stirred
    That, all uncouscious, twines above my window there.

Fair is the scene that meets the musing eye to-night;
  But morn may wake the battle's sleeping storm,
And when the day is done, another moon may light
  Another field of death, with furrows smoking warm!
June, 1862.

THE RUIN.

WHERE the stunted pines and scrub-oaks grow
  Desert by the inmates years ago,
A lone house stands on the mountain's brow,
The haunt of the snake and the scorpion now,

And a path-way yet may be traced in the sod
Long by the footsteps of man untrod,
And still on the spot where the garden has been
Are the tall blue-flag and the daffodil seen.

Hoary and lone in the sedgy old field,
By the dank undergrowth but half concealed,
The oaken doors have gone to decay,
And the window frames have fallen away,
But a lone rose strays o'er the open sill,
And a scattering peach-tree blossoms still,
Tho' none but the passing traveler now
Gathers the fruit from the silent bough.

The stagnant waters of a sunken rill
In the moonlight glimmer, white and still;
Where the head of the fountain used to flow
Moulders the moss-grown barrel below;
Undisturbed the gnats o'er the surface swim;
The green lizard crawls round the slimy brim,
While the sour crab-grass and the choking sedge
Are spreading around from the marshy edge.

Where the cheerful hearth was ablaze long ago,
The blackberries twine, and the thistles grow,
The blue-birds build where the loose stones fall;
The crickets chirp in the grass-grown hall;

THE RUIN.

And many a time, in the days of yore,
Might be seen the bats, a countless score,
Come forth from the thatch, in the twilight gray,
Where the weather-worn shingles had blown away!

But a wild storm came, and the Northern blast
Rude-shook the ruined walls as it past,
And the old roof fell in the tempest's din,
Startling the bats from their hold within;
And now the dismal owl alone
In state sits on the chimney-stone,
Or hoots from a neighboring gum at night,
When the sky is clear, and the moon shines bright.

On the hill-side bleak, where the brambles blow,
One grave lies apart, and three in a row,
The foot-boards have rotted, and the stones at the head
Record not the names of these slumbering dead;
Should you question a neighbor how they had past,
"The family," he'll tell you, "*moved out to the West?*"
They have gone toward the Sun, a new home to find,
And left not a trace but this Ruin behind!

MEETING OF THE SHENANDOAH AND POTOMAC
AT
HARPER'S FERRY.

HOW brightly glows yon azure summit's sun-crowned crest,
   Serene amid the vapors gathering there!
Along its misty crags the eagle seeks her nest,
   High soaring through the golden-tinted air;
While far below forever rolls the restless stream
Whose origin of old the Indian thought divine,
And deemed its glancing waters caught their starry gleam
From those eternal orbs in night's dark vault that shine.

MEETING OF THE SHENANDOAH AND POTOMAC.

Thou beautiful, wild River! thy fountains have their source
   'Mong far-off heights; and through Virginia's fertile vale,
As loth to leave the Blue Ridge side, still winds thy course,
   O'erswept by many a murmuring mountain-gale:
The wild deer quits the lonely steep thy wave to drink,
As twines thy jewel-threaded chain the hills around,
Blithe chirp the birds among the shrubs that line thy brink,
And sweet is heard the distant sheep-bell's tinkling sound.

All gently sway the quivering pines that fringe thy flow,
   'Mid blossoms gay, and bees thy waters wend,
While in the grassy meads beside, the grazing cattle low,
   The rustling corn, and yellow wheat-fields bend:
Ah! listing to thy dear, familiar sound again,
Soft as the shade of Summer-clouds upon thy shore,
Borne by the light breeze into the waving grain,
Come back sweet mem'ries of the days that are no more.

Losing thyself, at last, beneath the storm-swept height,
   Merged in the deep Potomac evermore,
The rifted rocks are rent asunder by thy might,
   As loud resounds the tameless torrent's roar;
A thousand echoes wake from cliff to cliff beyond,
A thousand ripples break from rock to rock beneath,
A thousand breezes bear on high the swelling sound,
And far the white foam, flashing, flings its crystal wreath.

MEETING OF THE SHENANDOAH AND POTOMAC.

Rush on, forever on, ye River, wildly grand!
   Tearing your pathway through the mountain's heart,
Whose pinnacles sublime seemed formed by Nature's hand
   To mock the puny works of human art!
And here will stand these mountains blue from age to age—
The eagle ne'er will lack her rock to build upon;
Forever roaring here, these stormy tides will rage—
Forever flow beside the tomb of Washington.

Rear your firm forms, ye Mountain-summits dark with shade!
   As calmly o'er your height the Sun goes down,
As when our great Immortal Dead beneath you strayed—
   The torrent thunders still as fiercely on!
For here the youthful Washington o'ertrod the shore,
And Jackson saw yon fringe-tree deck the margin green,
The Sage of Montecello wandered here of yore,
And from yon self-poised rock surveyed the glorious scene!

The Sun, whose golden strands across the ripples gleam,
   Shines on our homes destroyed, our lands laid waste;
While in our lovely Valley ruin reigns supreme—
   A black'ning record, ne'er to be effaced!
But free as are the skies above, these Streams below!
Nor war, nor ruin stays their wildly-rolling wave;
Their waters ripple on the same, although they flow
By many a wasted home, and many a hero's grave.

So rolled their current when the Indian's shadow dim
  Fell on their breast two hundred years ago,
And so will roll, perchance, when his last requiem
  Is chaunted by the vast Pacific's flow;
A thousand echoes will from cliff to cliff respond,
A thousand ripples break from shore to shore beneath,
A thousand breezes bear on high the rushing sound,
As far the white foam, flashing, flings its crystal wreath!

LINES TO A CEDAR OF LEBANON.

How lonely are those dark hills now,
  Vine-clad, alas! no more,
Where Jordan's stormy waters flow—
  How silent is the shore!

The rose of Sharon grows beside
  The Kedron's silver rill;
The lily drinks its crystal tide
  In dewy freshness still.

LINES TO A CEDAR OF LEBANON.

The cedar stands on Lebanon;
    The morning sun-beams rest—
The quiet stars shine sadly down
    On Galilee's cold breast.

Upon the desert mountain's brow,
    Where Jesus' footsteps trod,
Still waves the wilding olive-bough
    Above the hallowed sod.

But Judah's race is desolate,
    In ruins is their shrine,
While mosque and moslem desecrate
    The vales of Palestine.

Proud Salem sits a crownless queen
    Where once full-robed she stood;
At Zion's gate there still are seen
    White lepers—but no God!

But glory from on high shall gleam
    Upon those scenes now dim,
When o'er the darken'd skies shall beam
    The Star of Bethlehem!

OCTOBER MUSINGS.

I.

AGAIN thou comest, beautiful October!
With thy warm, rich hues, and soft-breathed airs,
Thy clear, cool mornings, and thy mellow hours
Of evening! And tender images of life,
And dreamy memories are in thy wake!

Soft as an infant's breathing, or the fall
Of distant waters on the drowsy ear,
Sweet recollections crowd upon the brain,
As, lost in tenderest reverie, our thought
Forgets the while to note the flight of time,
Till in the lonely silence of the wood,
Some ling'ring, plaintive bird bursts forth in song,
Or the wind's rustle through the colored leaves
Recalls the wand'ring mind to things around—
The melancholy murmur of thy breeze,
The softened beauty of the landscape's scene,
Of shining fields, and forests waving bright,
Ever dispose the musing mind to pensive Meditation.
But thy coming fills
Us now with thoughts far sadder than the season!

To think another battle season o'er,
The Autumn dawns upon our darkened prospects!
No, 'tis not alone the slow, but rich
Decay of blooming Nature that we're called
To mourn; the green groves perished in the pride
Of Summer! And henceforth their naked stumps
Alone remaining, with the fenceless fields,
Stript bare, translate a sorrow to the eye;
While sound, continual from morn till night,
The drum's loud beat, the tramp of horse, the march
And countermarch of armèd foes (a horde
Of licensed plunderers, still bent on conquest,
And the swift subversion of each right
To freemen dear), until the loathing ear
Is sickened with the everlasting din,
And the mind fevered with the thought it stirs!

II.

Again I see, with eye of phantasy,
The tranquil Rappahannock wind along
Its narrow course, between its cliffs of clay;
Its low sweet murmurs sadly chiming with
The wind-notes swelling, flow and fall away;
The wavy outlines of the snowy clouds
Glide with the ripple, and the blue-bright skies
Quiver in the clear wave's embrace, with many

A dimpled gleam. Heaven smiles upon the scene,
But the bare earth returneth not her smile!
And the lone river pours its deep lament,
In dirge-like melody along the vale,
In answer to the mute appeal of voiceless
Desolation, where the blacken'd walls
Alone remain, amid the waste, to mark
Where once there rose the hospitable roof
Of many a noble mansion, bowered in shade,
While wide the spreading vista Southward stretched,
And gay, green hill-tops rounding far away,
Were dotted o'er with many a verdant grove.
Once smiling harvests crowned these golden vales,
And generous youths, and blooming maidens gath'ring
Round each hearth, with peace and plenty dwelt:
Methought the broad earth knew no happier land!
Alas, alas! for thee, my Sunny South!
Bathed in the blood of thy devoted sons,
Thrice hallowed now for all thy wrongs, and all
Thy woes, we hold thee dearer still than in
Thy palmiest days!
     See, yonder, fire and death
O'erswept the valley; there th' invading legions
Dyed the gory tide! Ah! there too fell
The hero who set his petrific line
Of squadrons on, a wall of stone, to breast

The shock of battle! There fell he, the gifted,
Whose eloquence shall echo from the rostrum
Never more; and he whose sun-browned hand
His children's daily bread shall earn no more;
There youthful genius unrecorded died;
There victor and vanquished together sank;
Beside them stretched the quivering steed; and swept
The flames, devouring what the sword had left,
Till e'en the grass refused a single tuft
To wave above their common sepulchre!
Oh! man, vain-glorious boaster, that pretend'st
To rule the elements, calling thyself
Earth's lord—rearing thine unremaining temples,
Building mould'ring monuments of stone
Less fading than thy fleeting memory!
How the wind's sigh along the steadfast steep,
Standing where it hath stood since time began,
And the deep wave's murmur, mock thy babblings!
Th' eternal heavens glass themselves within
Its breast, while thousands of thy puerile race
Are melting like the morning mists beside!

III.

October, with his dyes, hath decked the earth
To be the tomb of thousands slain in battle!
The balmy Spring, the heats of Summer pass,

OCTOBER MUSINGS.

The sere leaf falls, the frost and snow return—
Death comes with all! The sword, the pestilence
Destroy their myriads! The stormy sea
Retains its spoils; the fierce volcano flames
Above the waste, where buried thousands lie;
Nor dies mankind alone; all living things
Must share their fate, and be no more remembered:
Monsters of the deep, beasts of the field,
The tender flowers, the forests, disappear;
The rocks, the ocean's shores, all waste away;
And cities fairly built, the nests of commerce,
Level with the plain are lowly laid,
Or lift their broken shafts, with hi'roglyph
Engraved, above the wreck of empire gone!
And genius—though the breath of fame revive
The mem'ry of the gifted and the great—
What see we of the *hearts* of those who sleep?
Let him who thinks he knows the hist'ry best
Of sage renowned, or hero, now compare
His knowledge of his brother here, who shares
His toils by day, his couch by night, with all
The thoughts, the waking dreams, the fantasies,
The smothered passions, and the vain desires
That make the life of his own secret soul,
Heard, seen, by none—and ask himself how much
Of all he hourly thinks and feels will e'er

Survive his fleeting breath? Which of the hopes,
The fears, the joys and griefs that make for each
Life's little sum, shall leave a trace behind?

IV.

As warmly beat the pulse of life in veins
Of Egypt's mummy kings, as in the heart
Of him who sways their broken sceptre now;
The builders of the pyramids were men,
As well, nor worse perchance, nor better than
The turbaned Turk, whose unprogressive foot
Treads out the flickering embers of the great
Light-radiating mother of the world!
Think'st thou that love, and sorrow, pain and pleasure,
Blend more intimately with the tide
Of human life, that floods the streets, to-day,
Of fashion's gay metropolis, than that
Which rolled through ancient Thebes, when the dark
    Nile,
Lit by a thousand lamps, bore on its breast,
Of old, the golden-lighted barge of her
Whose charms conquered the world's great conqueror?

The dim traditions of the past record
The rise, the progress, and the overthrow

Of mighty peoples; cities, in whose streets
The sea-weed grows, were once as populous
As powerful; as proud the merchant prince
Of Tyre as he who dwells beside the silver
Thames! The vale of Sodom blossomed as
The rose! The halls of haughty Nineveh
Once echoed to the joyful sound of harp
And timbrel, and the voice of melody.
And here in this so-called New World, where are
No palaces gray-grown and ivy-clad,
No tombs, relics of old magnificence,
No silent city of the dead, sunk in
The sea, or whelmed beneath the desert's sands—
Oh! more sublimely sad the thought! the share
Disturbs the ashes of a race whose story
None have writ, and none remain to write!
Yon grass-grown mound, scarce rising from the plain,
Is now a Nation's sole memorial!
Upon the field of Fredericksburg was found
An Indian dart beside a minnie ball—
But who shall tell us of the combat fought
There in another age? Or who shall say
No younger scion of a race unborn,
Straying beneath these skies at Summer's eve,
Shall there find some, to him, rude implement
Of war, and know of us and ours no more!

Where the bold hunter trailed across the breast
Of Alleghany, startling from their lair
The brindle panther and the catamount,
Two hundred years ago, the locomotive
Thunders round the curve, while far below
The village-spires are gleaming in the glen!
Two hundred years to come, and where will be
The men who throng the busy street to-day?
They who now ply the loom, or th' anvil clang,
Or he, the traveler, passing through their midst?
Each has his friends, his occupation, and
His home—so had the dwellers upon earth
Before the flood! They ate, and drank, and slept;
They married, and were given in marriage;
They built and multiplied, and waxèd great;
Then came the floods, the rains descended, and
They were not—they, nor their habitations!
Still shall they slumber on with all that die
Hereafter, till the angel's trump shall sound:
Then, too, thy graves, America, unmarked,
Or well adorned—both mound and monument—
Shall open; and the secrets of thy lost
Inhabitants at last appear: and they
Who fell on yesterday, and they who slept
As well long centuries ago, the dead
Of ages far remote, together rise!

V.

God of eternity! how vainly seeks
The soul, upon this perishable globe,
For some faint symbol of stability,
Wherewith to paint its poor conceptions of
Thine ever-during reign!
      Go pierce yon mount
Whose feet, rock-sandaled, press upon the plain,
And see whereon its firm foundations rest;
And say from what abyss of ocean, or
From what unknown volcanic crater was
Its vast form heaved in some revolving throe?
When lived, when died the reptile saurians
Whose monstrous track is graven on the rock
Within its bowels? Where wert thou, O man!
When bloomed the borders of the Frozen Sea,
With more than tropical luxuriance?
And what convulsion wrecked so fair a realm,
Yet left the impress of its withered weeds
To last when thou, and all thy works are gone?
Go count the leaves that wave in yonder wood,
And mark the thousand microscopic forms
That live and breathe on every leaf, and breed
Their generations in a day, till night
Bring dire destruction, and their world undo—
And form a just conception, if thou can'st,

Of all the living things that now exist,
Or dead that have existed!
                    Unnumbered is
The starry host that treads the floor of heaven.
And science, but the art of naming them,
Knows not their multitude; nor knows she aught
Of that broad zone of milky light, stretching
Across the sky, studded with stars on stars
As thick as pebbles on the beach. Within
Its glittering maze, seen by the telescope
Alone, are loop-holes in the sky, wherein
We catch a glimpse of shining heav'ns beyond,
Starry as those of ours, with realms of light
Perchance that dazzle our Sun's eye, as he
The eye of man. Farther than thought can reach,
It may be, endless space is peopled with
Pure beings God creates to worship Him.
Yet from the vault of heaven have vanished stars,
And some appearing on a sudden shone,
And for brief space increased, and then decreased
And disappeared, as with a burning flame
Blazing and going out—light-giving suns,
For aught we know, more bright than ours—leaving
A train of worlds in darkness to expire!
Nothing we know or can conceive but that,
If matter, is destructible. All change,

And all are subject still to dissolution
And decay. The Great First Uncreate
Alone had no beginning, hath no end—
God only is eternal, and with Him
No shadow is of turning or of change!

And what are we but weary dreamers, steering
Toward the dark unknown abyss of fate
As constantly as yonder rising star
Moves onward to its setting in the West?
Thy course, Capella, we may trace, but who
Shall tell me mine! What mockery is human
Grandeur! Oh! how vain is wisdom's lore
To solve the problem of our destiny!
Treading continually the confines of
The viewless—groping on the darkened shore
Without a line, or measure, wherewithal
To sound the unknown waters ere I plunge—
Another state, that is not life, presents
Itself, and I—not I that know myself,
The living I—but I that am about
To be—I know not what, a disembodied
Spirit—seem to stand alone, apart
From aught beside—an atom in the ocean
Of infinity! an atom, yet
Immortal fragment of the Universe!
Father of Light and Love! Creator! Thou

Who hast of old the earth's foundations laid,
When all the fading symbols of this Earth
Are perishing around us, and the heavens
Themselves wax old, and, like a garment, as
A vesture to be changed—O, what were man
And all his hopes, could he not look to Thee!
Relying on the firm assurance of
Thine everlasting promises, look forward
To the soul's eternal home, where the dim
Yesterday, of which we nothing know,
And the far-off to-morrow, bright and boundless,
Pass into the living Now?

VI.

O, call
It not an idle art to garner up
The best and brightest gifts of God to man,
All fleeting though they be, and tainted with
The dark primeval curse, yet emblems still
Of fadeless life, and joy's perennial bloom!
'Tis this that lifts the mind above the grosser
Elements of clay, by which it is
Encompassed, till it recognize within
The palpable, and visible, the essence
Of the spiritual, and unseen

But present aye! This paints the angel-shore
As bright and beautiful—far off, yet near!

We know not but our birth may be the kindling
Of a spark, long quenched in brighter spheres—
In realms of light beyond the unseen stars—
That thus are shrined within us beauty still,
And pathos, though without us be the cold
Hard world, and Brazen Age that moults within
The crucible of Use all finer types
Of things, and symbols of old poesy.
And this perchance is why we ever long
To reach the unattainable, but never
Find the soul's ideal in the real;
Nor wealth, nor power, nor pleasure, nor all
We know or dream of earthly good, though they
May satiate, can ever satisfy.

Ye are the idlers! not the poets—ye
Who tread beneath utilitarian feet
The morning dew-drops of the finer arts,
And e'en the flowers of God on which they hang!
Who think this world alone is worth a thought!
To whom this transitory state, with all
Its fading facts, appears more real than
Eternity itself! Dull worldlings who
Plod on your path, with narrow minds, eyelids

Ne'er raised from earth, cramping the brow,
Benumbing all the sensibilities,
Hard'ning the heart for love of sordid gain :
The deep truths underlying all we know,
Which human reason can not delve below,
Nor finite grasp the infinite—these, these
Have never entered your philosophy !
In vain for you God writes sublimest words
Upon the book of Nature, and imprints
His record on the soul; your opaque minds
Give no reflection back of that bright world
Upon whose very cope and verge you tread !
Your footsteps even now are echoing
Along the brink, and yet ye hear no sound,
Although Creation's varied tongues proclaim,
By day and night, their origin divine,
And all her myriad wheels in wheels revolving,
In their flight unworn, since first their wond'rous
Course began, through endless space resound !

VII.

The God who lit the living flame of man,
Of beast and fowl, of fish and insect mite,
Hath also tinged the sapphire skies above,
And fixed the different glories of the stars !
He decorates the coral caverns of

The deep, tuning its choir of wind and wave,
And voice of gentler sound, of crystal spring,
Of breeze, and bird, and bee, to hymn His praise ;
Framing the eye to see, the ear to hear,
And kindling in the human breast the love
Of lovely things, the quenchless thirst for knowledge
More exalted, and a purer life,
That man, though fall'n, immortal still, may long
For infinite perfection, and aspire
To reach the light of Heaven's eternal beam!

VIII.

Methinks the bards of latter days forget,
Amid their intricate obscurities
And fanciful conceits, the noblest end
And aim of Poetry hath ever been
To purify the fountain-springs of life ;
To elevate the thought, and to instill
The principles of truth, and in the soul
Awake a yearning for the pure, the good,
The beautiful—oft condescending to
Beguile with simple song th' unlettered ear
Of toil-worn poverty—teaching the young,
In earnest tones, the ways of wisdom ;
Painting vice foul, virtue fairer still,

So that the heedless may take warning, and
The timid persevere in doing well.

The older Bards were wont to kneel to Nature!
Priests of the woods and fields, they ever taught
The soul to recognize its Maker in
His works. The grandeur of this outward world,
Of sky and cloud, and snow-capped peak, to them
Was but the faint reflection of the glory
Of the inner light that filled their breasts
With holy joy! The tempest's thunder, and
The restless surge's muttered moan, were but
God's oracles, whose deep interpreters
They were! Earth's wide-spread plain, and her green
    hills,
With eagle height, and deeply cloistered dale,
The heaving ocean and the hurricane,
And the blue, boundless depths of starry space,
The human heart, with all things old and new,
Seen and unseen, within the scope of man's
Immortal mind, supplied a field to them
Exhaustless still for contemplation grand,
And God-like aspiration! For to the
Rapt soul, afflate with true divinity,
All things are full of poetry and song!
And though there are some virgin spirits born

Organic harps, mute but to God himself,
Which keep their incommunicable tones,
With vestal purity, for Heaven's ear;
Though breathing thoughts and burning words
Too oft exhaust the vital spark; and finer
Spirits, in a world of suff'ring, thrill
To sorrow's touch far oftener than to joy's;
Yet, yet would I, O Lyre Divine! might I,
Pour out my soul in one impassioned strain,
Then pass with the ebb-tide for aye away!

Patriotic and National Poems.

THE LAND WHERE WE WERE DREAMING!

FAIR were our nation's visions, and as grand
　　As ever floated out of fancy-land;
　　　　Children were we in simple faith,
　　　　But god-like children, whom nor death,
Nor threat of danger drove from honor's path—
　　In the land where we were dreaming!

Proud were our men as pride of birth could render,
As violets our women pure and tender;
　　　　And when they spoke, their voices thrill
　　　　At evening hushed the whip-poor-will,
At morn the mocking bird was mute and still,
　　In the land where we were dreaming!

And we had graves that covered more of glory,
Than ever taxed the lips of ancient story;
　　　　And in our dream we wove the thread
　　　　Of principles for which had bled,
And suffered long our own immortal dead,
　　In the land where we were dreaming!

THE LAND WHERE WE WERE DREAMING.

Tho' in our land we had both bond and free,
Both were content, and so God let them be;
  Till Northern glances, slanting down,
  With envy viewed our harvest sun—
But little recked we, for we still slept on,
  In the land where we were dreaming!

Our sleep grew troubled, and our dreams grew wild;
Red meteors flashed across our heaven's field;
  Crimson the Moon; between the Twins
  Barbed arrows flew in circling lanes
Of light; red Comets tossed their fiery manes
  O'er the land where we were dreaming!

Down from her eagle height smiled Liberty,
And waved her hand in sign of victory;
  The world approved, and everywhere,
  Except where growled the Russian bear,
The brave, the good and just gave us their prayer,
  For the land where we were dreaming!

High o'er our heads a starry flag was seen,
Whose field was blanched, and spotless in its sheen;
  Chivalry's cross its union bears,
  And by his scars each vet'ran swears
To bear it on in triumph through the wars,
  In the land where we were dreaming!

THE LAND WHERE WE WERE DREAMING.

We fondly thought a Government was ours—
We challenged place among the world's great powers;
    We talk'd in sleep of rank, commission,
    Until so life-like grew the vision,
That he who dared to doubt but met derision,
    In the land where we were dreaming!

A figure came among us as we slept—
At first he knelt, then slowly rose and wept;
    Then gathering up a thousand spears,
    He swept across the field of Mars,
Then bowed farewell, and walked behind the stars,
    From the land where we were dreaming!

We looked again, another figure still
Gave hope, and nerved each individual will;
    Erect he stood, as clothed with power;
    Self-poised, he seemed to rule the hour,
With firm, majestic sway,—of strength a tower,
    In the land where we were dreaming!

As while great Jove, in bronze, a warder god,
Gazed eastward from the Forum where he stood,
    Rome felt herself secure and free,—
    So Richmond, we, on guard for thee,
Beheld a bronzèd hero, god-like Lee,
    In the land where we were dreaming!

As wakes the soldier when the alarum calls,—
As wakes the mother when her infant falls,—
    As starts the traveler when around
    His sleepy couch the fire-bells sound,—
So woke our nation with a single bound—
    In the land where we were dreaming!

Woe! woe! is us, the startled mothers cried,
While we have slept, our noble sons have died!
    Woe! woe! is us, how strange and sad,
    That all our glorious visions fled,
Have left us nothing real but our dead,
    In the land where we were dreaming!

And are they really dead, our martyred slain?
No, Dreamers! Morn shall bid them rise again;
    From every plain,—from every height,—
    On which they seemed to die for right,
Their gallant spirits shall renew the fight,
    In the land where we were dreaming!

Unconquered still in soul, tho' now o'er-run,
In peace, in war, the battle's just begun!
    Once this Thyestean banquet o'er,
    Grown strong the few who bide their hour,
Shall rise and hurl its drunken guests from power,
    In the land where we were dreaming!

THE BATTLE OF BALL'S BLUFF.

SILENCE rested in the Loudon Valley's breast,
    Silence slept upon the hill,
When the crimson sunset faded in the West,
    Silent was the scene and still,
        Save the Potomac's roar.

Marshaled in their pomp at eve th' invaders stood—
    They had come to crush the free!
And they dreamt not there, beside the rolling flood,
    Their last requiem should be
        The wave-beat on the shore.

Calm their sleep, and long—but ere the morn awoke,
    Blazed the lurid fires of war—
Like the fierce tornado's crash, the battle broke
    On the startled slumberer's ear—
        The live shot rattled o'er.

Thicker, faster still, the deadly volleys fell,
    Dark'ning the air at dawn of day;
And wild there rose above the din the Southron's yell,
    As the black clouds rolled away,
        Along the trembling shore.

Ere another sun had set upon that wave,
  Death had met them in the vale,
And their dripping ranks were gathered to the grave,
   Blending with their dying wail
      The purple river's roar.

Of the shatter'd wreck swept down the Bluff below,
   Few return'd their tale to tell;
And the leaves of Autumn shed a redder glow
   In the valley where they fell,
      To rise again no more!

In their pride at eve they stood; now cold and low
   Falls the dew on each dumb breast;
Deeper is the silence by the river's flow—
   Stiller is the soldier's rest,
      On the Eternal Shore!

MY HEART IS IN THE MOUNTAINS.

———

RIGHT nobly flows the River James
    From Richmond to the Sea,
And many a hallowed mem'ry claims,
    And tribute of love from me;
But Western Tempe farther on—
    Mother of limestone fountains!
My heart goes back with the setting sun—
    My heart, my heart is in the Mountains!

There where the fringe-tree nods his plume,
    Beneath the white-pine's shade—
There where the laurel drops his bloom
    O'er many a wild cascade—
There where the eagle seeks his nest—
    Mother of limestone fountains!
List to an exile's prayer for rest—
    My heart, my heart is in the Mountains!

The wide expanse of the boundless sea
    Is a sight to stir the soul,
And there is a breadth of majesty
    In the Western prairie's roll—

But give me the heights that milk the clouds,
    And gather the dew in fountains!
Give me the peaks, with their misty shrouds—
    My heart, my heart is in the Mountains!

There's something blank in the landscape here,
    And tame in the water's flow—
I pine for a mountain atmosphere,
    And a crag in the sunset's glow!
King of the Hills! Blue Ridge that I love!
    Feed still the Vale with fountains,
From rock and dale, and mountain-cove—
    My heart, my heart is in the Mountains!

SONG OF THE SOUTH.

CHOIR.

SING us a song for the Land we Love!
    O! Minstrel, sing us a song!
Let it be sad as a mateless dove,
    But make it not, Minstrel, long!

On his viol a master's* mother breathed
  The latest sigh from her mouth ;
Oh! thus on thy harp, with cypress wreathed,
  Catch thou the breath of the South!

For the citron shall bloom in the orange grove,
  And the muscadine twine as of yore,
But her Darling Dead, embalmed in her love,
  Shall return for their fruit no more!

Then tuning thy harp o'er the fresh-turned sod,
  'Neath a bough where the raincrow sings,
Catch the breath of the South, like the spirit of God,
  Poured over thy trembling strings!

MINSTREL.

The Song of the South—with her free flag furled!
  My harp grows mute at the prayer!
For the anthem would trouble the heart of the world,
  Like the song of a falling star!

  For they should remember that 'twas not alone
    'Gainst the odds of her Northern foe,
  That she struck when the star of her victory shone,
    Or sank in her hour of woe!

*Paganini.

Then, Choristers, pardon the mournful chord,
    For the hope of our country fled,
The dream of her glory dispelled by the sword,
    Her laurels encircle the dead!

So I'll hang my harp o'er the fresh-turned sod,
    On a bough where the raincrow sings,
Till the breath of the South, like the spirit of God,
    Pour over my trembling strings!

JEFFERSON DAVIS.

[There is an aged lady in Virginia, an octogenarian, who has seen two revolutions, or rather two developments of the same revolution—that of '76, and that of '61. Ever since the inauguration of JEFFERSON DAVIS, this old lady has regularly summoned her household at 1 o'clock each day to offer up prayer for the President of the Confederate States; and notwithstanding the fall of the Confederacy, and the imprisonment of Mr. DAVIS, regarding only the *de jure* aspect of affairs, she rings out her bell daily at 1 o'clock, recalls the family around the domestic altar, and offers prayer for the President of the Confederate States. She declares she means to continue this practice—sublime in its devotional simplicity and faith—until the end of the term for which he was elected.]

IT is not Grant, nor Sheridan, nor Sherman
    Hath blanched the whitest truths on hist'ry's page,
But such as thou with this thy grand old sermon,
    Imprinted on the forehead of the age—

That with God there's no *de facto:* only right
  Can make a president or fill a throne,
That prison-bars, tho' they foreclose the light,
  Debar not titles nor obscure the sun.

Foul fetters bind not justice down, because
  A tyrant forge or rivet them, forsooth;
Barbarian orders are not more than laws,
  Nor brutal outrage more than simple truth.

Therefore, Mother in Israel, lift thy prayer,
  Thy President, because he cannot die,
Despite the worst that Vandal vengeance dare,
  Is safe—his term is immortality!
August,·1865.

ODE

Recited at the Consecration of the Stonewall Cemetery, and Reinterment of the Brothers Turner and Richard Ashby, at Winchester, Virginia, October 24th, 1866.

I.

HARK, hark! I hear the booming cannon's roar!
  Each murd'rous blast, the startled echoes mock!
The bomb-shells burst, the fiery hailstones pour,

The earth beneath my feet, the solid rock,
　The very air is shaken with the shock;
And in the furrows of the battle plain,
Red blood is streaming thick as Autumn rain,
And agonizing cries go up to God, in vain!

Forward! for all that's dear—for home and hearth!
　Fling out the battle-flag, and strike once more
For freedom, and the land that gave us birth!
　Sound, sound the drum, and let the cannons roar!
　Thousands of brave men marching on before,
To Him whose name our country's stay shall be,
　Now look—the God whom all of us adore,
Who calms the storm, and rules the raging sea,
Will guide us yet to peace, through glorious victory!

II.

Vain, vain! th' unequal contest, worse than vain!
　Vainly our prayers besieged the highest throne;
Vainly our blood flowed out upon the plain—
　Against a world in arms we stood alone!
As some rude hunter, from a towering oak,
　O'erlooks the vale, and views the herd below,
　Lets fly his darts, and lays the foremost low,
So fell our leaders by the fatal archer's stroke!

And lo! there galloped through the gate of war,
    Two brothers riding side by side, with spurs,
And nodding plumes, and swords that gleamed afar,
    And eyes like day, when first the sun appears.
They strode their steeds as Neptune strode the sea,
    And mane to mane they bounded through the vale,
    Like some harmonious rhythmus on the gale,
And smiled at danger, as more brave than he.

Their long black locks encharmed our southern wind,
    Which left the orange bloom, and golden maize
To follow them, though often left behind—
    The milkmaid on the heifer leaned to gaze.
One fatal morning laid the younger low—
    No more by rattling hoof of his, the fawn
    Was startled as she browsed the hill at dawn—
No more his bugleblast struck terror to the foe!

His brother dead, like Leda's Joveborn son,
    On milk-white steed among the Argive youth,
Th' Ashby, 'mid his southern comrades shone,
    Craving one immortality for both;
Full oft at dawn Potomac saw him nigh,
    His beard upon his charger flowing free,
    (A black swan's wing upon the frothy sea,)
The war-gaze filling all his dark romantic eye.

By eve the fount far up some Hampshire dell,
    Laughed in the snowy fetlocks of his steed!
The star-begotten river knew him well—
    Oft broke his image on her rocky bed;
And Tuscarora, with her maiden mien,
    Swerved toward the horseman as he rode beside,
    Silent as she, and deeper than her tide,
As knightly form as ever water-nymph had seen!

Stern only to the foe, his name a spell,
    Won on the soldier hearts and made him dear—
Till off the edge of War the Ashby fell—
    Dropt from the cope, and went out like a star!
Here lie the Twain; their epitaph be this:
" These Brothers struggling one just cause to gain,
    Full-breasted both upon the foe were slain,
And now together sleep, in one sweet dream of peace!"

They are not Death's—relinquished all his claim!
    Their deeds to History and immortal Song.
Their souls to God, their memories to Fame,
    Their ashes to Virginia belong!
Sleep Heroes—with no weight but flowers, sleep!
    Your mother, like the Osprey, makes her nest
    For you with feathers plucked from her own breast,
Here on the border of the eternal deep!

The struggle o'er, no shaft of triumph looms—
  The laurels of Virginia are but here!
Bound on no temples save these white-browed tombs,
  No victor crowning but the Sepulchre!
And yet they die or wither nevermore!
    But live, while shines, a gem of God, one star
    In any crown of peace, or sounds of war
One note, and bloom till Memory's self grows hoar!

Methinks, from off yon mountain-crest, the pines
  Will sprigs of evergreen waft on the gale;
Methinks the Western sun, as he declines,
  Will span with glory's prism all this vale,
An arch of triumph, and an arc of peace!
  Methinks I hear the genius of the State,
  Out on th' impassioned atmosphere relate,
In tones of lyric pathos, burning words like these:

III.

Thrice welcome, war-scarred veterans, who alive return!
  Ye vowed to do your duty—well ye kept your plight!
Sleep well, my dead, till History inscribe your urn,
  Though conquered, victors still, though not triumphant—
    right!

My heroes slain, my prophets martyred one by one—
    My banner trailed in dust—but never tire 'mid all!
Ye braves! these fallen forms shall up again and on
    Through all the coming years, made glorious by their fall!

The stars shall rise that shine into the souls of men,
    And in mysterious junction, dominate the earth!
The suns that blazon liberty shall burn again,
    And light the fires of glory, over freedom's birth!

IV.

Thus speaks the grand old mother of us all,
    Her voice still reaching for th' ethereal spheres—
Her heart on fire, a battle-flame her soul,
    Her eyes ablaze, like the eternal stars.
We hearing, listen to the voice of Heaven,
    From out these clouds of tyranny and shame,
    Look up, take heart again, and name the name
Of some far Sabbath, which to liberty is given!

A day shall come perchance—a morn shall dawn,
    Shall give each grave a tongue, to every tongue
A text, to ev'ry text a sacristan,
    An altar, and a priest, from whom the young
Shall learn the sermons of these darling dead,
    To teach them how to dare, and do, or die,
    To save the fruits of peace, or vainly try—
But failing, leap to war, as groom to bridal-bed!

THE VIRGINIANS SIT AND WEEP.

[Super flumina sedimus et flevimus.]

FROM where thy waters lip
   The sea, proud River James, to where
They sparkle in the mountain air—
Beneath our gray old temple-shades,
From Jamestown to Montgomery's glades,
   The Virginians sit and weep.

   Majestic as thy sweep,
Potomac, where thy waves move on
Beside the tomb of Washington,
The current of Virginia's grief—
On Vernon's Mount, Immortal Chief,
   Thy Virginians sit and weep!

   Shall stranger sickles reap,
Great Jefferson! where thou didst sow,
While thy Rivanna's murm'ring flow,
At Montecello's base, to thee
Complains that now, no longer free,
   We Virginians sit and weep!

THE VIRGINIANS SIT AND WEEP.

    Smooth was thy face, and deep—
All radiant, but not with joy,
And beautiful as the Spartan boy
Agesilaus loved; but look!
John Randolph! on thine own Roanoke,
    We Virginians sit and weep!

    From where, Kanawha, leap
Thy headlong waters into birth,
To where the rich and kindly earth
Pours out upon thy broad'ning breast
Her oil—thou Oxus* of the West!
    We Virginians sit and weep!

    Ozark! grim and steep,
Look eastward to the Chesapeake;
Thro' all this vale our sorrows speak—
From Piedmont to the Sewell's chain—
Ohio to the ocean's main,
    We Virginians sit and weep!

* The ancients declared that the Oxus was covered at times with a film of oil; a similar appearance presents itself on the Kanawha.

Tintographic Melodies.

CALIDIA.

I.

TIME, thou canst never restore me
    The rapture which crowned me a king,
When Calidia melted before me,
    A charmed and an idolized thing—
    A maid in the bloom of her Spring.

Her voice, seraphically maiden,
    Seemed to fall from the spheres on high,
Like the sweet silver bell music-laden,
    Which the falcon transports to the sky,
    Full oft when the hawkers are nigh!

Of sap, like the aspen, her form full,
    Was tremulous still as its leaf,
And she gathered her bust in an arm-full,
    As the harvest-maid gathers her sheaf—
    Her girdled and shattering sheaf!

But doubt not her spirit was stainless,
    Because with much fervor it glowed,
The stream of her love, while it drainless,
    As the Shannondale fountain, flowed,
    Was pure as a smile of God!

And her breast, while swelling as finely,
    As Corregio's cunningest skill
Hath made Magdalena's, divinely,
    Like that of the painter's ideal,
Reposed on the Bible still!

And Time, thou canst never restore me
    The rapture which crowned me a king,
When there rose, like a vision before me,
    This maiden, an idolized thing,
    All fresh with the blush of her Spring!

II.

One evening (how well I remember!),
    We stood looking up at the Moon;
'Twas one of those eves in September,
    That ever are fading too soon,
    When we stood in the moonlight alone.

We had stepped from the porch, where the vining
    More than half intercepted the light,

To a spot where the Moon, in her shining,
    Was clean, and immortally bright,
    In the still, solemn temple of night.

And you would have had, if you'd seen us,
    A sermon instead of this rhyme,
Although there was nothing between us
    Save faith, yet that is sublime,
    When pure and unsullied by time.

Ah! would that Time could restore me,
    Like flight to the caged eagle's wing,
The faith that I felt when before me,
    There rose, an aerial thing,
    This maid in the bloom of her Spring!

III.

I asked her to sing; she dissented;
    But, after a blushing or two,
When I asked her again, she relented,
    As virgins are fond to do,
When lovers persistently woo.

Her voice, though in compass defitient,
    In soul was exquisitely fine;
The music was hers, quite sufficient
    To make *me* think it divine,
    While the words they were poor—but were mine.

CALIDIA.

SONG.

In the Spring the partridge pairing,
    Sees the thrush build in the haw,
And the maid's complexion clearing,
    Soft she sighs, "Ah! me," and "Oh!"
    Oft she sighs, "Ah! me," and "Oh!"

When the Summer comes more warming,
    Then she loves to dream alone,
And her reveries are charming,
    But she's fickle as the Moon—
    Yes, she changes with the Moon!

When the Autumn berries color,
    And the vintage stains the wold,
If you love her, haste to tell her,
    For she'll listen now when told—
    Ah! she'll listen now if told!

Mark me—in the still September,
    When the Harvest Moon's above,
Dare to touch her hand—remember
    Now's the full tide of her love—
    Lo! the full tide of her love!

Though she's sweet in Indian summer,
    If you love her, don't delay!

CALIDIA.

For the frost will overcome her,
 And in Winter she'll say nay—
 Sure in Winter she'll say nay!

She ceased, and no voice like the maiden's,
 Methought, as it haunted me there,
Had ever in silvery cadence,
 Died away on the still night air,
 So mournfully, musically clear.

And oh! what a world of religion,—
 What a spell that I dreamt not before,
Came down from the moon-gilded region,
 And taught me to love her and more,
 And bade me my spirit outpour:

Till my words grew unmeaning, but tender;
 They were low, they were idle and vain;
But her own heart had taught her to render
 The sense mine failed to make plain,
 And she sighed—was it pleasure or pain?

I vow that I never have known it!
 I heard but that tremulous sigh,
While the maiden, her figure all moon-lit,
 Held a tear, like a star, in each eye—
 The reflex of stars in the sky!

And oh! if Time could restore me
    The rapture which crowned me a king,
When I saw thee, Calidia, before me,
    A charmed and an idolized thing,
Dear Maid, in the blush of thy Spring!

IV.

We parted, I scarce know the reason—
    'Tis fitting that dreamers should part!
But 'twas due more to chance and the season,
    Than due to my will or her heart—
    'Tis fitting that dreamers should part!

Not a star is there less in the heaven—
    Not a voice of the night is less clear,
Not a tint is less gorgeously given,
    When each rose-leaf is wet with a tear,
    And sun-kissed, the morning is here.

But ah! the sweet sanctified seeming,
    That wrapt them in splendor and gold,
Was due to the dream I was dreaming,
    And my lover-like fancy of old—
    Magician with power untold!

And the threads of this fanciful dreaming
    Are broke in my heart—in its core,

CALIDIA.

And love, with his old saintly seeming—
    His power and freshness, is o'er,
His music an echo—no more!

Will no voice seraphically maiden,
    And less from the earth than on high,
Like the silvery bell, music-laden,
    Which the falcon transports to the sky,
    Enchant me again ere I die?

Can no sight, I care not how fleeting,
    No vision in beauty arrayed,
No eye-glance in extatic meeting,
    Nor the glist of an aureoled head,
    Arouse me as one from the dead?

Nay, Time! thou canst never restore me
    The rapture which crowned me a king,
When bright, like a vision before me,
    Rose a maid, as an idolized thing,
    All flush with the blush of her Spring!

NIVEAN.

I.

SHE spoke not of love, for she dared not,
    Though her gray eyes were flashing the truth,
I broke not of love, for I cared not,
    My heart was at home in the South—
    My heart was at home in the South!

But this heart will be cold in oblivion,
    This heart must be cold at its core,
When I forget radiant Nivean,
    As she sped o'er the crystaline floor,
    Wing-footed, a fairy, and more.

A gift, (how divinely 'twas given!)
    To the snow from Ireland's sun,
To Erin herself from Heaven,
    Yet in all save a sweet Irish tone,
    Her being was Canada's own.

Short and warm as the summers her breath,
    Like the nights were her beautiful eyes,
Her cheek to her neck was the path
    Aurora, with rosiest dyes,
    Treads down from the boreal skies.

NIVEAN.

Her brow it was Bel-œil mountain,
    And her mouth it was Ha! Ha! bay,
Her soul a Laurentian fountain,
    But the rapids her love—nay, nay,
    In passion Niagara's play.

But she breathed not of love, for she dared not,
    Though she tasted the thought in her mouth,
And I spoke not of love, for I cared not,
    My heart was at home in the South,
    My heart was at home in the South!

II.

I spoke of our men and their deeds,
    Till her Irish heart wept at my story;
But I chid her, and told her the sceds
    They had sown on the battlefield gory,
    Would blossom in harvests of glory.

She questioned—right timidly truly—
    Of our fair, and a kindling light,
Breaking over my features unduly,
    As th' Aurora breaks out on the night,
    Told more than I wished to her sight.

And I know not what impulse diverted
    Our feelings, now pensively grown,

That I sang, with my features averted,
    To an air not-inopportune,
    This hymn to a Southern Moon:

From thy full quiver, Dian, shaking,
    Light arrows falling, gleam afar;
In my heart I feel them breaking.
    They prick me to a nameless yearning,
That I were radiant as a star,
    And set in heaven bright and burning!

Thine arrows tangle in the moss,
    Whose folds from yon live-oak depend—
They come and go, and are a loss:
    But, tell me, are they lost for aye,
Or, like Christ's figures in the sand,
    Will they be gathered by-and-by?

The Indian-jasmin opening hails thee,
    The Southern orange, with perfume
Denied unto the Sun, regales thee;
    And thus there are of souls who faintly,
On the light of day presume,
    But at night are sweet and saintly!

Majestic, passionless, serene,
    Come teach me thy philosophy—

O ! teach me all I should have been !
    When passion's fountains, overfull,
Waste idle tears, O, let them be
    A lunar rainbow of the soul !

But methinks, (and I frankly confess it,)
    That my song was higher than she,
For she laughed as she could not repress it—
    (Her laugh was ever to me,
    Like sunbeams athwart the sea !)

But she spoke not of love, for she dared not,
    We were troubled to silence both,
For I broke not of love, for I cared not,
    My heart was at home in the South—
    My heart was at home in the South !

III.

Now Venus looked down upon Mars,
    And Mars stood away for the Moon,
Who fled through the nebulous bars
    Of light, while the stars aboon,
    Were fleeting with silvery shoon.

Burlington bay lay congealed,
    As smooth as a marble floor ;
The wind blowing o'er his field,

NIVEAN.

Had swept it from shore to shore,
    As gleaners the threshing floor.

'Twas Carnival night at the Rink,
    And I sandaled her feet with steel;
She must have been blushing, I think,
    For my trembling hand would reveal
    The emotion I wished to conceal.

And this heart will be cold in oblivion,
    This heart will be cold at the core,
When I forget radiant Nivean,
    As she sped o'er the crystaline floor,
    Wing-footed, a fairy and more!

"But Nivean," I whispered, "uprisen
    In beauty, the Moon's increase
Makes the Rink itself like a prison—
    Let us fly to the Night, ere we miss
    The joy of his luminous peace!"

So we stole from the Rink to our sleigh,
    Her small soft hand in mine,
Unobserved from the Rink away,
    Where the mirth effervesced like wine,
    To the night—a holier shrine!

NIVEAN.

Away o'er the snow, away,
    To the music of tinkling bells,
With their merry-wild interplay,
    Away over heather and fells,
    Away through the frosted dells!

Away o'er the snow, away!
    Far over the creamy hills,
While the ice, like dashing spray,
    Round ocean-fretted keels,
    Flew up from the iron heels.

Away o'er the bay's smooth floor,
    Where the bird at our prow took wing,
And our well-shaped sleigh drew o'er
    Full many a frozen spring,
    Like any swift-pennated thing!

Way out on Ontario far,
    Our silvery snow-shell shone,
Like the Mother of Love in her car,
    When the golden reins fall down,
    And the strengthless doves speed on.

And we laughed, this maid and I,
    For we knew we were all alone,
And we warmed to the tender sky,

NIVEAN.

And felt for the pale, cold Moon—
But Spica Virginis shone!

And this star of celestial birth,
With its tutelar mission large,
I vouch as my witness to earth,
How safe I returned my charge,
On Burlington's icy marge.

For I broke not of love, for I cared not,
Though never more tempted, in sooth,
And she breathed not of love, for she dared not,
Though her gray eyes were flashing the truth—
Her gray eyes were flashing the truth!

IV.

How the orange buds in unfolding,
Teach us soft and delicious things!
Th' impregning gales, through the wolding,
Flutter low, with voluptuous wings,
In the face of our warm, Southern Springs!

The Winter had passed with its gleaming,
Its quarto bound up in the year,
Of the Canada maid but a dreaming,
A sigh and a silent tear,
Remained to my heart of her.

'Tis thus that she wept when we parted—
    I gave her a chain golden-wrought,
With a symbol of pearl twin-hearted,
      And my hand in her dark hair caught
      As I wound it about her throat.

She took from a cage above her
    A bird of varied plume—
A bird she had tutored to love her:
   "He was born in meridian bloom,
    Take him back," said she, "to his home!"

When the Winter had passed with its gleaming,
    I stood where my heart was at last,
By my side all radiantly beaming,
      In the beauty of joy unrepressed,
      Was the angel my soul knew best.

And I drew from my breast warm and tender,
    My bird with an ill-defined pride,
But lo! (and I tell it with wonder,)
      When he looked on the maid at my side,
      The sweet warbler fluttered and died!

And 'tis true that she wept when we parted—
    And would that her gift I'd denied;
But I dreamt not that thus broken-hearted,

LORA LOGIE.

At being divorced from her side,
This warbler had fluttered and died.

And it seems to me now as a warning—
I fear, and I cannot tell why,
On the bourn of some fair summer morning,
Like this bird of meridian sky,
My own heart will flutter and die!

And would I had broken and spared not
To my Canada maiden the truth—
That I spoke not of love, for I cared not—
My heart was at home in the South—
My heart was at home in the South!

LORA LOGIE.

SOFTLY and tenderly,
    Lora Logie,
Falls the night-melody
    Over the sea;

LORA LOGIE.

And over this sea of years,
Ruffled by raining tears,
Float, through a mist of fears,
    Echoes of thee!

Faintly and fitfully,
    Lora Logie,
Mournfully, constantly,
    (Ah, me! ah, me!)
Notes like the bell-bird, still,
Or the weird whip-poor-will,
Follow me, fit to fill
    Sad memory!

Hintingly, hauntingly,
    Lora Logie,
As vespers mellowly,
    Musically,
Out from the convent bell,
Ave Marias swell
For the dead day . . . ah, well,
    Lora Logie!

UNDERNEATH THE FULLNESS.

I.

UNDERNEATH the fullness
   Of thy flood of mellow light—
Underneath the paleness
   Of thy presence, Queen of Night,
   Floats a vision radiantly bright—
Floats a vision that my soul entrances,
Lapt in almost heavenly hues and fancies.

II.

And I see a gentle spirit's whiteness,
Like yon moon-lit cloud's unspotted brightness,
   While her eyes of clearest gray,
   With their sweet, untroubled ray,
Speak a mind whose peace and lightness
   Naught can dim, or take away!

III.

With a nature innocent and guileless,
   And a heart forever young,
Oft her spirit's melody out-gushing
   Through the liquid ether rung,

Still the mocking-bird provoking
    Wild to warble as she sung—
Oh! the freshness of her gentle presence
    Stealing my worn thoughts among,
Thrills my bosom like the breath of spring-tide
    O'er the breast of Nature flung!

TO MISS NANNIE B*****.

WHAT star presided at thy birth,
    Beneath whose soft, celestial spell,
Down-trembling to the charmèd earth,
    The very soul of music fell?

Like Echo, or young Sybalis,
    Or note preserved from Orphic plaint,
Thou art a Voice, sweet Cantatrice,
    Thy physique but a supplement.

As all the tints in mingled throng
    Produce White Light in purity,
So all the elements of Song
    Combine to form thy minstrelsy.

Priestess elect of Melody—
    Eldest and dearest of the arts—
Wed Music still to Poesie,
    Before the altars of our hearts.

And lift our souls to ecstasy,
    Until from hearing thee we're taught,
That Song's akin to prophecy,
    A far diviner gift than Thought.

EGLANTINE.

SLEEPS the shadow on the water,
    Stays the wind upon the hill,
Waveless are the weeping willows—
    All is silent, all is still.
Silence lingereth in the valley,
    Broodeth o'er the deep ravine,
And forever, and forever
    Thou art silent, Eglantine.

EGLANTINE.

Lingering by the Shenandoah,
    When the sunset died away,
Dreamed I of a maiden fairer
    Than the lilies of the May.
Now the lily, blooming lowly,
    Scents the field and churchyard green,
And the stars are shining purely
    On the grave of Eglantine.

Faintly smile, O, Alcyone!
    In the dim, uncertain blue,
Never more shall twilight, trembling,
    Love's sweet trance for me renew.
Wake, ye slumbering hearts of violets,
    Soft your purple bosoms lean—
Balmy as your blowing petals,
    Was the breath of Eglantine.

Sing, O saddest bird of evening!
    Ever-mournful whip-poor-will,
Gone from me are dreams elysian,
    Grief alone my breast can fill;
Sweeter than all joy, and dearer,
    Tender tears to me have been,
Tears of wildest melancholy
    Rained o'er thee, my Eglantine.

EGLANTINE.

Spirits bright as thine are rarely
   Left to light this lower sphere,
And the links were loosened early
   In the chain that bound thee here,
Where thy voice's quivering cadence,
   Clear as fountains crystaline,
Seemed an echo from the star-strand
   O'er the river, Eglantine.

Rose-bud lips, alas! how chilly,
   Angel footsteps passed from earth,
And a fairy form that faded
   Like a dream of heavenly birth,
Haunt my heart with lovely image,
   And a youthful maiden mien,
In the sadness of my spirit,
   Stealeth o'er me, Eglantine.

Damp the sod where dust is crumbling,
   Cold the form the clod hath pressed,
But with thee is peace eternal,
   Strife nor sorrow stirs thy breast.
Though the mound lie mute and coldly,
   Yonder in the churchyard green,
Thou hast past the heavenly portal,
   Pure and gentle Eglantine.

THE FLOWERS WE CALL FLORA.

THE flowers we call Flora . . .
  My Flower is darling Lora!
    But her real name 'tis not:
For the name of her face is Beauty,
And the name of her soul is Duty,
  And the name of her mind is Thought!

The morn we call Aurora . . .
My Morning I call Lora!
  But her real name is Love:
For whate'er on earth we name her,
As Love will the Angels claim her,
  A saint in the sky above!

THE PICTURE.

YOUR frame is all the atmosphere!
      Methinks
I see the canvas penciled clear—
    "God *pinx*."

Bright picture of the past, uneye
    My soul!
Or fade, or change, or melting, die
    Or fall

Down to my arms, or grant that I
    May too
A tintograph, lie on the sky
    With you!

Your frame is all the atmosphere!
    Gold links
Suspend you to the heaven, where
    Methinks
I see the canvas penciled clear—
    "God *pinx*."

CORINNE.

I.

PASSIONATE Corinne!
    Voluptuous, dark, and dreamy-eyed,
With flowing tresses, black as midnight's stillest hour!
The creamy flower, the heavy-hanging orange flower,
  That odorous droops o'er Arno's classic tide,

Had lent thy brow its pure and pearly charm—
  The self-same sky, with warm and generous glow,
  That gilds the citron-apple bending low,
Moulded to grace thy ripe and rounded form,
            Beautiful Corinne!

II.

  Beaming, bright Corinne!
The mellow air of purple-fruited vales,
  The viney vales of soft-skied Italy,
  Breathed o'er thy cheek the burning blush,
  Caught from her sunset's gorgeous flush;
The moon-beams lit thine eye, whose quivering sails,
  In shadowy light, play o'er the Ionian sea—
            Peerless, proud Corinne!

III.

  The flame that lit thy poet-soul divine,
  Caught on the altar and consumed the shrine:
Thy life was brief, but bright, and ere its setting sun,
For thee the goal was reached, the glorious triumph won;
  To stifle, in the sealed cells of thy breast,
  The eloquence of feelings unexpressed,
Conscious that folded in its prison-clasp of clay,
The early germ of genius wasted day by day—
  This, this was not reserved for thee,
  Daughter of storied Italy!

To love was thine, and be beloved, in vain—'twas well!
Thy life's ripe fruit and not its blighted blossom fell!
    In the freshness of thy fame to die,
      Crowned beneath thy Rome's unclouded sky,
And closed with thy high destiny—was it not time
To make thy love immortal, and thy woe sublime,
              Glorious Corinne!

LUCILE.

I.

CHASTE and meek Lucile!
    Thine eyes were soft as violets dipped in dew,
    And folded in the hollow dell,
Long-lashed and drooping, deep and blue;
Thy red mouth mocked the scarlet-blowing bell,
    That dangles 'mong the dusky fern;
    Thy cheeks like morning tints that burn,
      Flushing oft and quickly pale—
      England's Lily of the Vale!
              Loveliest Lucile!

II.

Fairy-fair Lucile!
Like sunshine in thine Ocean-Isle,
    Thou didst but faintly smile;
But the breath of burning Italy
Could never thrill a fairer form,
Her sunny skies ne'er lend to thee
    A richer, rarer charm,
        Exquisite Lucile!

III.

Tremulous Lucile!
Thy voice as silvery soft, as faintly low
    As the rustling piney blades
    In the far-off mountain-glades;
Thy foot-step fell as lightly on the lea,
    As falls the plumy flakes of snow,
    That mutely meet the cloudy sea,
        Shrinking, shy Lucile!

IV.

Delicate Lucile!
Dew that feeds the snow-drop's bell
    Was ne'er more stainless in its purity,
Than, brimming in thy soul's seal'd cell,
    Thy love—a fountain, full and free,

Forever flowing—flowing onward to the main,
As streams that seaward go, returning not again;
O! silent, seeming passionless Lucile!
Thy mute and songless lips reveal
No murmur of the clanging strife
That marr'd the music of thy life,
Sensitive Lucile!

'TWAS IN THE GENTLE TWILIGHT SEASON.

'TWAS in the gentle twilight season, long ago,
 I strayed beside the waters of this lovely stream,
And, as I listened to the ripples' murmuring flow,
 Wove many a fancy wild and golden-tinted dream.

Still idly lingering, gazing on the sparkling wave,
 I saw the young Moon kiss his brow from realms of light,
And as he smiled to greet her soft embrace, hope gave
 To all my glowing thoughts a hue as fresh and bright.

And thus I deemed life's star-lit stream should bear me on,
 While hope should light my path, and faith should guide the way,

Until love's triumphs crowned, ambition's laurels won,
  My bark should reach, at last, the light of clearer day.

Still gaily o'er thy breast, fair Stream, the starlight gleams,
  And as I stray beside thy water's murmuring flow
Will come again the fancies wild, and golden dreams
  Whose brightest hues have past away long, long ago!

MARY.

I HEARD three lovers once dispute:
  One said thou wert a Flowret; one
Maintained a Dream; the third, Ripe Fruit:
  At length said all: "God knows alone:

"We only know if flower, or maid—
  If budding girl, or girlish bud,
An involute most sweetly made—
  She's surely something fresh from God!"

O, SWEET AT MORNING'S DEWY DAWN.

I.

O SWEET at morning's dewy dawn,
    The wild bird's warbled lay,
Ere yet the yellow-rising sun
    O'erspreads the rosy day;
But sweeter than its melody
    And fresher than the dew,
Thy memory comes back to me
    Across the mountain's blue:

II.

And oft I stray where we two strayed,
    By quiet vales and streams:
Or resting in the fragrant shade
    Beneath the flickering beams,
Fond thoughts take flower-shapes for me,
    As by-past scenes appear,—
My musing heart communes with thee
    And feels thy presence near.

III.

And when the Moon sheds tranquil light
    Along the dusky steep,

And trembling shadows, faintly bright,
    Float o'er the silent deep—
What time the night-hawk calls his own,
    And stars to stars reveal
The destiny of worlds unknown—
    Then elfin fancies steal

IV.

From out my folded heart's retreat
    To dance by mem'ry's beam,
As from the rose's, fairy feet
    Dance by the fire-fly's gleam—
Fond thoughts take flower-shapes for me,
    As by-past scenes appear,
My musing heart communes with thee,
    And feels thy presence near!

MY THOUGHT GROWS HAZY WITH THE SEASON'S TOUCH.

MY thought grows hazy with the season's touch:
    For this is Indian Summer, loved so much
By bards, who set to most mellifluent rhyme
Their hymns to Nature, in the olden time.

The sun, a day-born moon, shines dim through smoke;
The crows that clamor in the wilted oak,
  With many a darting and defiant mawk,
  Move not the ruffles of the lordly hawk.

The driven shingles, echoing o'er the hills,
Betoken care for coming Winter's ills;
  Only the red-bird's left to greet the morn—
  At eve, the wain brings in the golden corn.

The thirst to *see* thee—simply *see*—no more!
Comes like some new and un-named passion o'er
  My soul, and makes it gloomier than the mist
  Which steals, like unformed dreams, from out the West!

O! LORA, AS THE EARTH PURSUES.

O LORA, as the earth pursues
  The Sun by his own light,
One-half illumed, one-half in hues
  Of dark, despairing night,

So I pursue thee, through, me seems,
    Of life the hollow sphere,
Sometimes aslant beneath thy beams,
    Sometimes direct and near!

With twilights following radiant noons—
    Conjunctions and eclipse—
With early and senescent moons,
    From depth to depth I lapse!

A SERENADE.

ALONG the steep the filberts' tassels swing,
    The silver-maples' purple clusters blow,
Upon the rocks the honeysuckles cling—
    The matted moss is pink with bloom below.

Spring's touch renews the sap and wakes the flowers,
    With thrill and gush of sunlight and of song.
Come, Love, from thy boudoir, and seize the hours
    Too flush with April joy to linger long.

Arise, my Love, and leave thy virgin couch,
   Like some sweet dryad from her dripping urn:
The fair young Morning, with her coral touch,
   Makes all the hills and vales to blush in turn—

The Morn sits at her wheel a coralist,
   And sprinkles over cloud, and mist, and sod,
Her rosy dust, and cries: "Fair Reverist!
   Awake! come forth, and join our hymns to God!"

THE WIND CHIMED LOW BY THE DEEP WAVE'S FLOW.

THE wind chimed low by the deep wave's flow,
   As I strayed with my blue-eyed Lora,
And the twilight's gleam fell over the stream
   Of the winding Tuscarora.

O softer far than yon pale star
   Was the melting glance of Lora,
And her voice, like a bird, through the stillness stirred
   The dream of Tuscarora.

Now the Whip-poor-will is repeating still
   His chant to Pan or Flora,
But in fancy oft a sound more soft
   Floats over Tuscarora.

THE SOLITARY HORSEMAN.

I'VE heard, sir, from the village mouth,
   You go a journey to the South,
Toward Mont Blanc and Chamberry,
   Where father went in Napoleon's day,
To a southern land called Italy,
   I scarce know where, but far away.

And here is a casket, gentle sir,
With a billet-doux and a lock of hair;
For it may chance that you shall meet
   A horseman clad in sombre gray,
With features sad, but mild and sweet,
   I scarce know where, but far away.

He rides a black but star-browed horse,
And urges him with gentle force;

I know not whither, for being sent
　　By me, without intent, (O, me!)
He rides across the continent,
　　I fear to perish in the sea.

I did not think that he'd depart—
I dearly loved to try his heart:
And if he knew that I repent,
　　Though on the borders of the sea,
He'd ride across the continent
　　But he'd come back again to me.

The moons return . . . so does not he;
His face is south, his back to me,
And cruel is my punishment.
　　Jesu, Maria, pardon me
For sending o'er the continent
　　My love to perish in the sea!

And by every one that journeys south,
I, hearing from the village mouth,
Inclose him word that I relent;
　　For I fear unless he hears from me,
He'll ride across the continent,
　　And perish in the farther sea.

THERE ARE PRECIOUS CARGOES STRANDED.

THERE are precious cargoes stranded
    On a bleak and barren shore,
Where the billows, silver-sanded,
    Break amid the tempest's roar!
There were forms that now are sleeping
    Where the sea-weed tangles o'er,
Veiled from eyes that long were weeping
    For the lost that came no more!
Hence it is, Majestic Ocean,
    We hear plainings and a moan,
When thy waves, with gentle motion,
    Ripple where the wind has blown!

There are thoughts we utterly rarely
    In our heart of hearts the same;
There were hopes we cherished early,
    Ah! and names we never name!
There were ties that have been nearer,
    Broken now and passed away,
And a love that once was dearer
    Than the fancies of to-day!

Therefore 'tis that viewless faces
    Haunt the solitude around—
Therefore 'tis the spirit traces,
    Through the stillness, noiseless sound!

OUT ON THE SEASHORE.

O WHAT a world breaks on the sight,
  In early morn, or wakeful night,
    Out on the Seashore!
A line of blue, like level hills,
A briny breath the ether fills—
    Ever, evermore,
      Out on the Seashore!

Monsters! Sceptres! Cities gone!
Islands buried! Fleets undone!
    All on the Seashore!
Yon line of blue is a sepulchre!
Only the Mermaids prosper here,
    In their Boudoir,
      Out from the Seashore!

St. Agnes of Guienne:

BY

DANIEL BEDINGER LUCAS.

ST. AGNES OF GUIENNE.

IT chanced one season when the lush young vines
    Did yield their purple globules to the touch
Of rural maidens, mellow as the wines
    Of Ischia, rosy, sparkling, troubling much
The heart of man, that, as the custom went,
The Guienne vintage closed in merriment.

The viol (old Cremona's fashion,) sings
    Sweet as the birds of Southern everglades;
But sweeter still the rustic laughter rings
    Through aisles of beauty, lining olive shades,
Where glancing ankles sparkle in the whirls
Of dance, like jewels in a maiden's curls.

As some old skiff that hath not known an oar
    So long the moss grows on the slimy keel,
Struck by a sudden wave from almost o'er
    The sea, obeys the impulse, and with reel
And lurch, strains at the mooring chain—
Struck by a wave from almost o'er the main—

So some old dames, with uncouth step and check,
    Taught in their early youth and beauty's prime,
Break in the dance at some young mocker's beck,
    But soon exhausted, yield the floor to time,
And to their daughters, as the winter's snows
To sunshine's joyance at hoar March's close:

And on the borders of the ring there stand
    Grandfather's gray, (old venerable vines!)
And priests, and crownèd Ganymedes who hand
    The goblets flush with purest-strained new wines,
While deep embossed in shade glide lovers who,
All unperceived, would fain steal out of view.

The dance being o'er, it was not strange, in sooth,
    A slender form, round-ripe with all, was seen
Bending—soft-bending—towards a comely youth,
    Who led her homeward through the clover green:
Two neighbors these; a sweet, French maid, Hermine;
The other Claude, a youth with manly mien.

Her voice was the sweet principle of oil;
    Within her eyes, pure-gushing founts whence flowed
In crystal currents, fluid light and soul,
    Young Love in fairy barks of myrtle rode
At ease, or flashed the spray from gleaming oars,
Which drove the ripples to their dark-fringed shores.

And sweet, imperious Eighteen, the time
   When Nature hurries every rosy charm
Into the full-flushed glory of its prime
   Had bursted every blossom of her form:
She wept at times, then chided her own fears . . .
A simple bird's-nest troubled her to tears!

That night Claude slept beneath her father's roof—
   His chamber next the sky, alone, apart;
Gay music still was in his ears, the woof
   Of silver-threaded fancies spun his heart,
Inspired by many a goblet's rosy sip,
And steeped—too deeply steeped—in love, for sleep.

How strange, inconsequential, are our dreams!
   One would have thought that genially would flow,
Like gentle currents of meandering streams,
   His visions, flush with April joy—but no!
He dreamt a hurricane, a rudest breath
Of monsoon, threatened all with instant death!

It seem'd to lift the rafters, and to spin
   In eddying whirls the thatch's straw on high!
And yet, up through the roof, he thought, was seen
   The stars and moon unclouded in the sky:
(Awake, asleep, such are our dreams through life—
Strange contradictions, mingling peace and strife!)

He thought, warned by the crash that threatened sore,
    Deeming the house must fall, he rose and traced
The shaken wall, and walked the trembling floor,
    To find some portal of escape with haste,
Improved by fear, but with such tangled weight
As dreams aye clog upon the sleeper's gait.

Now, foliated in her double gown
    Of night, by female fancy deftly planned
In strange volutions, which, while gazing down,
    The angels oft desire to understand,
Hermine, also, had rocked her golden head
On restless pillow of her virgin bed.

It chanced, too, she bethought her, much as would
    Become a maid, upon her lover's fault
Of walking in his sleep, and by what mode
    His mother told he should be called to halt—
By wordless handing of some object o'er,
Which seeing, he straight following, was secure.

Thus, wrapping him about with sweetest fold
    And tissue of her pretty maiden fears,
She scarce had gi'en her lids into the hold
    Of sleep, when on the balcony which rears
It's roof alevel with her Eastern light,
She heard a footstep on the arching height!

Her pulse grew still with fear, her bounding heart
    Forbade her list'ning by its own impact—
But Love, a weird magician, with his art,
    Supplied what strength her nature else had lacked:
Like some white dryad from a fountainhead,
Out from the couch's tapestry she fled.

Her loose sleeves hung about her snowy arms,
    As upward bent they raised the Eastern blind,
Whence, springing to the balcon, with alarms
    Full-blooming in her timid maiden mind,
Her lily feet, fanned by her drap'ry, flew,
Dousing their snowy whiteness in the dew.

And O! too sure the Moon, with fleecy girth,
    Threading her mazy pathway through the sky,
And pouring day-like splendor on the earth,
    Upon the balcon painted to her eye
Her lover, walking slant, and near the verge,
O'er which his downward step were death to urge!

Now summon all thy strength, pale, tossed Hermine!
    With present-minded tact, outstrip the dread
That threatens him, and lead him through the skein
    Of something handed him, that he, being led,
May follow as an angel might, astray
From Heaven's gate, didst thou but lead the way!

Nay, nay; but what? lo! guiding, guardian sprites,
  That tend the steps of youth to keep from harm,
And ye, chaste stars, and all celestial lights
  That bind our fate by influential charm—
What shall she hand? Around, above, beneath,
Is blank of objects, and delay is death!

As Venus, rising o'er the orient waves,
  Down shook the milky foam in spumy robes,
From saffron locks, and pinkly rounded eves
  Of lustrous chin, and softly shaded globes—
So moulted, without effort, as it seemed,
The maid her outer vesture snowy-reamed.

The stars 'gan twinkle with a newer light—
  The Moon flung cloudlets o'er Endymion's eyes,
Who sat beside her in the car, and bright
  The proffered robe shone blanching to the skies!
But whiter she, save where her blushes waft,
Like sunrise flushing on some Parian shaft!

And as the Parian quarriors' lamps once shone
  Through fractures of the rock, of pinkish hue,
And creamy strata of the peerless stone,
  Far flashing o'er its spars and veins of blue;
So Claude's bright eyes, through glancing shade and
      night,
Flashed o'er the marble of Hermine their light!

A sudden change enveloped all his dreams,
   As well there might . . . he thought the storm gave up
Its heaving spirit, and with chastened beams
   A new-born planet, bursting through the cope,
Waved sattellites at him—diviner things
Than new-young moons, or Saturn's golden rings!

He followed as it were on wings new fledged—
   The earth repelled his feet, dropt off their clogs
As when before the sun, all fiery-edged,
   Down sinks the murky weight of heavy fogs:
The figure he pursued, with light afar,
Now seemed to glimmer, now to sparkle near:

Then through a fissure in the sky it leaped—
   A touch but burned his eager grasp and glowed,
While all its vesture from its shoulder slipt,
   He seizing, was divine—a mantled god!
But yet the light was gone—the storm seemed o'er,
And back to his couch, (as he was wont), he bore.

He thought he folded round him as a zone,
   A soft young virgin planet's starry robe,
And that ethereal passion, never known
   To man since from the deep God drew our globe,
Poured warmly into most voluptuous depths,
And heaven-dewed kisses touched his thirsting lips.

He dreamed, and seemed to know it was a dream,
    And nothing thought it strange this maid, or star,
Should interchange its being—sometimes seem
    Hermine, Hermine at times a heavenly sphere :
Sometimes his joy blushed at itself; then all
Was poetry—fruition of the soul !

He wished to dream for aye ; but dreams of bliss
    Are swifter-pinioned than the tufted grouse ;
A little noise—a whir—a gleam, or less—
    A glancing plume through sombre shade . . arouse,
Arouse, thou sleeper! for thy dream hath power
To haunt a life, but not to stay an hour !

And O ! the mystery of his wakened thought !
    There was the robe, and on it worked 'Hermine,'
Frilled at the top, in front, at bottom wrought
    With careful, scolloped hems and stitches thin—
To Claude a mystic leaf all sybil-wove,
By happy winds waft from what nymphic grove ?

From out this labyrinth no thread gave vent,
    And ere one thought was hatched another shook
The shell of incubating wonderment—
    The flight one doubt, eschewed, another took.
Grieved at his fate, (that he had lost a star),
Claude claimed and kept the robe it seemed to wear.

Next morn Hermine was sick, her mother said,
  Because she trod unwisely all the sets
And measures of the dance upon the mead,
  And paid the cost of pleasures in regrets.
Claude saw her not, and pondered more the white
Enfolded meaning of the robe-of-night.

Ah, well! in such a jealous world as this
  Love can not thrive: within his bower the spies
Who guard but to betray his dream of bliss,
  Are legion, and the stars themselves have eyes!
A rustic moving on his path along
Had seen what, understood, were nothing wrong.

Upon his neighbor's terrace, dressed in white,
  Two forms—or ghosts, or flesh—that night had seen,
Which were so loving close that not the light
  Of any star could he discern between:
But by the crescent of the Moon that shone,
He would be sworn one was Claude's father's son.

In vain the struggle of young Innocence
  Against the current of unjust surmise!
Suspicion's tide, by hint and inference,
  Grew like a mountain-source from pouring skies,
Until the stream quite overbore Hermine . . .
Sweet witch to float in such a sea of sin!

A parent, too, the rustic was, and felt
   A touch of interested duty moved
To tell the father of Hermine her guilt,
   And vouch the story which his eyes had proved,
And straight, unsparingly a tale impressed,
Which stirred a tempest in the father's breast.

For Hermine's father, from his youth to prime,
   Had borne his portion in Italian wars;
The fire of glory burned beneath the rime
   Of age, and courage vouched him by its scars;
He grasped anew his weapon in his ire,
And swore the vengeance of an outraged sire.

Poor Fawn! what could she say? Is it not true
   All that the conscientious neighbor speaks?
Can she face down the simple truth, or mew
   The tell-tale blushes of her crimson cheeks?
Can she divert suspicion from her fame,
And swear no lover to her chamber came?

Alas, the woven thread of circumstance
   Was destined to a still more tight'ning woof;
For while Claude slept one morn, a casual chance
   Drew there his mother, and she saw the proof
Beneath his pillow, of the maiden's sin—
A robe embroidered with her name: "Hermine!"

ST. AGNES OF GUIENNE.

'Tis sad—'tis very sad to think upon,
   That Fate should drive two blameless souls apart;
But, whate'er else is new beneath the sun,
   The record of a broken human heart
Repeats itself, from age to age— sung o'er
From Eurydiké down to lost Lenore!

With cruel hand the age's sophistry
   Pointed all sorrowing maids to convent-gates,
Whose hinges turned like ports of destiny,
   Closing behind them and their loves and hates,
With solemn vastness, mausolean gloom,
For sorrow simple death, for sin a tomb.

And gliding hither, Hermine pledged her will,
   To leave behind her name, her heart, her troth—
(Go to! for God was over-ruling still—
   A maiden's prayer out-weighs a giant's oath!)
One morn a voice relaxed the Abbey-door
Saint Agnes built, and Hermine was no more.

There rose, with turrets questioning the air,
   This Abbey of our Mother of the Snow,
Built by a Franco-Spanish maiden fair,
   With Gothic courts and oblong portico,
And just a dash of Mooresque fantasies,
The legend of whose origin was this:

Rich in that poverty the world calls wealth—
 More rich in every jewel of the soul—
Rich in sweet grace of maidenhood and health,
 In noble rank, in virtue more than all,
Fair Agnes dwelt upon the broad Garonne,
Within an antique castle of her own.

Being won by art gallant, she loved a knight
 Less honored than the king, but only less;
The pride of courtly circles, and delight
 Of women, for his high-born gentleness—
She loved him with a famished love, though strong,
Doting as angels dote upon the young.

This knight engirdled with his wooing arm,
 Pure as Diana's moon-lit belt, her zone,
And tasted from her mouth the budding charm
 No manly lips had sipped before his own:
But in the end—alas, for honor's school!—
Betrayed her woman's love and trusting soul!

Deserted, broken hearted, paler than
 The veil of mists that over glaciers rise,
Young Agnes wept, and her sweet sorrow ran,
 Washing the starry pupils of her eyes
With ceaseless tears, till, pitying her grief,
The Virgin bore upon her wings relief.

Maria came, crowned with the glorious Sun,
    Treading upon the Moon, whose silver horn,
'Lumed from herself above, was pointing down
    To where fair Agnes slept and rivalled morn
In sweet perfection of transcendent grace—
Her curls, like mists, encircling her face.

' Fair maid,' the Virgin said, ' thy prayers are heard;
    And I, Mother of Mercy and of Grief,
With knowledge of the founts of pity stirred
    In the Eternal Heart, will find relief,
Daughter, for thee, and teach thee what behest
Fulfilled shall bring to thee the balm of rest :

' When in the morn thou wakest, look abroad,
    And where thou seest first a fleece of snow,
Take thou thy wealth and institute to God
    A Convent, where, as Brides of Christ, may go
Young maids, who, like thyself, shall dearly prove
The anguish, folly-born, of earthly love.'

Thus spake the Virgin Mother, and although
    The Summer Solstice, now in even scales,
Held out the night and day, a flake of snow,
    Across the pine-tops of some Eastern vales,
Upon a high-majestic hill was found,
Crowning green grass as em'rald waves are crowned.

ST. AGNES OF GUIENNE.

Here, on the margin of a glassy Bay,
    Fair Agnes built, with Gothic taste and skill,
A Virgin's claustral home, where she and they,
    Elect of Christ, and tempered to His will,
Clothed on with charity, relieved and blest
The poor, and gave themselves to God and rest.

'Twas chiefly at her own desire, Hermine,
    A gentle Novice, sought their sisterhood;
Her beauty veiled, her love concealed within
    These sacred walls, which still a trophy stood
Unshook, through centuries elapsed, to show
The mercy of our Mother of the Snow.

Yet, Hermine's earthly love pulled at her zone
    Like starving infants at a mother's breast;
And oft, like Eloise before the stone
    Of giant altars, where her vows were prest,
A flash of memory touched her thoughts to fire,
And filled her soul with a renewed desire.

A staid, sweet sadness settled on her brow—
    The dreamy depth of her blue eyes increased—
Her clear, fresh mountain-rill of laughter now
    Lay motionless within her virgin breast;
At noons, when all the courts her sisters filled,
She stood apart and watched a swallow build.

Mourn on! sweet, darling turtle-dove, mourn on!
  Mourn matelessly, sad, silent turtle-dove!
Mourn on in claustral sadness, and alone!
  Thy heart, though still the throne of human love,
Is known of God, and He (but only He!)
Is greater than a woman's sympathy!

Mourn, thou, sweet turtle, mourn! no nuptial moon
  Shall measure bliss unbounded through her flight
For thee, nor, round with silver joy, lay on
  The sky her horn upon thy bridal night!
No orange-blossoms, white as early snow,
Shall young companions garnish round thy brow!

And Claude? Ah, well! 'twas his no less to mourn:
  Down through the thick blue curtain of despair,
His waning eyes gazed wistfully and lorn,
  As through the offing, peering into where
The dark, full misting sits upon the sea,
The shipwrecked sailor gazes from the lea.

And often through the calm and solemn night,
  Rounding some cape, or steering 'twixt two isles,
His eager eye swept toward the Convent light,
  And letting go the oars in dream, the whiles
He floated purposeless, with hands conjoined,
His rod relaxed, his bait by fish purloined.

The Autumn trode upon the Winter's skirt;
  The Winter lined with frost the robe of Spring;
Sweet May, her head with violets engirt,
  Filled Nature's lap with vernal blossoming,
While inward set the tide of sea-like love,
Till breeding flocks and mating shepherds throve.

One eve a quiet clothed the water's breast;
  In stillness slept the mellow-breathing air;
A flame of gold burned through the couchant West;
  In the dark aisles had died the vesper prayer:
The sun came dropping, like a gymnast, by
His arms, as 'twere, from cloudy bars on high.

The mists had hung their ruddy films upon
  The coast at morn, and would not up nor off;
Yet rolled the Basin's waters smoothly on—
  A shallop's sail could scarce find breeze enough;
The fishers through the offing to the sea
Gazed, auguring a storm, and hugged the lea.

One hardy gondolier had ventured where
  The Basin, broadened, merges in the Bay:
'Mal Bay,' the sailors christen it, in fear,
  Because what time its treacherous waters lay
Most smooth, without a word, they swell and surge
Like waves which totter on the ocean's verge.

This shallop Claude's: above it, toward the sky,
  And dominating far and wide the plane,
A cliff reared up his craggy head on high,
  And flung his shadow 'thwart the level main,
Like some gigantic, dark-edged style, elate
Above a burnished silver dial-plate.

A white-winged dove, Claude's shallop sits, asleep!
  The troop of vulture Winds, upon the crest,
The signal given, plunge down on the deep,
  And plane the waters smooth upon his breast,
For leagues around, with sudden-rising roar,
Startling the birds that scream along the shore!

Resentful of this onslaught from the West,
  Quick flung the Bay his mad defiance back;
With deep, hoarse murmurs from his solemn chest,
  Upheaved his mane, and thundered on his track;
Lashing himself to silver-fretted froth,
Majestic as the Heavens in his wroth.

Tall firs bent o'er the beetling crags their plumes,
  And down, and twigs went drifting through the air
In mad career of dance, and whirl, and glooms
  Deep-settled, like the shadow of despair—
Claude's bark, a jockey, dressed in scarlet, still
Rode Neptune's horses with equestrian skill.

ST. AGNES OF GUIENNE.

Born on the brim of waters, and with storm
    Familiar as a child to nurse's mood,
He summoned to his aid, without alarm,
    What forces of security he could—
Let down his sail, flung out his too much weight,
And faced, with blanchless brow, the storm and fate.

Sometimes he scudded like an arrow cast
    Athwart the bosom of the hoary sea;
Sometimes he rode upon a billow-crest,
    Whither his tiny vessel seemed to be
Poised on the point, revolving as it were
A plate upon a necromancer's spear.

With lusty stroke Claude steered, and not in vain,
    On toward the Convent light, which, like a star,
Or burning pharos, lit the boisterous main,
    To guide our mariner across the bar
Into the Basin's far more stiller hem,
Where sheltering coasts and shoals would haven him.

With lusty stroke he battled, till apace
    With brooding wings more sober night drew on:
The hidden stars peered out upon the face
    Of heaven, through cloud-rifts peering one by one,
Like frightened quails who leave the sedge to see
The fowler gone, then call for company.

ST. AGNES OF GUIENNE.

And Dian shook her silver sceptre high
   Above the wave, and o'er the continent,
Flinging the clouds like fillets through the sky,
   Athwart the fields of azure firmament;
While Claude, reclining on his tired oar,
Less steered than drifted toward the quiet shore.

Into a curve of grayish coast exposed
   To the full Moon, above the willow-tops,
Where loving languor motionless reposed,
   As on the marge the lily's golden cups,
Now faint, his contest with the sea well o'er,
Claude drew his bark upon the quiet shore.

Not distant lay, by willows hid from sight,
   An Inlet from the Basin's shoal, yclept
The Bath of Saints, because herein, at night,
   In shadow of the Convent wall were dipt,
Immaculately kissed by saintly airs,
White model-artistes for the plastic stars!

Here often Postulante and Neophyte
   Unveiled their beauty to the conscious Moon,
Deep-shrouded in the mystery of night,
   And, with their virgin pureness clothed upon,
Gladdened the waters with angelic grace,
Till outer waves fought those within for place.

And hither oft soft-sighing Southern airs
    Would leave the jealous lilies motionless
To follow Hermine, whiter than the stars,
    Her beauty shrouded in a bathing-dress,
(O! mystery divine in purity!)
From silver shoulder down to ivory knee.

Water for her was welcome as the sky!
    A child she threw herself upon the Bay,
As do young sea-birds ere they learn to fly,
    And swam by impulse natural as they—
As fluttering their wings they scatter oft
The spray, she threw her pearly hands aloft.

Her breast shaming the foam that kissed and gloated,
    Her smooth arms buffeting the am'rous streams,
She in the music of swift currents floated,
    As a young spirit threads the course of dreams—
(Poetic dreams, which silvery spirits throng
On diamond feet, to wake the nerves of song!)

Into a curve of grayish shore outside
    This Bath of Saints, by accident, Claude rowed,
And drew his bark, whose Rhenish keel had tried
    The Basin's fury, and the storm outrode,
Upon the beach, and blessed the solid strand,
As exiles just returned, their native land.

His feet scarce touched the beach, till fervently,
   His eyes still fixed upon her Convent light,
He thanked the Snowy Mother, for that she
   Had saved him from the terrors of the night:
'Mater Nivalis! benigne! ave!
Star-eyed! to save men from the hungry Sea!

'Thou shelterest not me alone, but one
   More fair, for whom grape-clustering Guienne
Increased the margent of her ripening sun,
   And whom I dearly loved, alas! in vain!
A virgin pure as nested doves which bring
Travailing mothers to thy shrine in Spring!'

Thus he: was it the plaintive, weird-voiced wind
   That sighed through treillage of the muscadine,
And left an utterance of pain behind,
   Low-thrilling through the clusters of the vine,
Intoning, like a human voice that grieves—
Low-thrilling through the vines and willow-leaves?

He listened in a strange suspense of will—
   He doubted 'twas his fancy overwrought;
But so distinct a sigh of pain gave still
   Its stationary voice from out one spot,
That, prompt t' alleviate distress, he rose
To seek the source of such soft-wooing woes.

Beyond the willow's marge, upon a plot
    Green with the velvet of a richest sward—
No shrubs—no other flowers—on a spot
    Clean as the sky—there lay, ill-starred,
A maiden form, that, melted, might have been
Poured in her bathing robe of spotless sheen!

And all her beauty flourished at one glance
    Upon his stricken and poetic eye;
'This is,' said he, 'a pleasant dream, perchance
    From Earth the transit to Eternity,
And yonder form Elysium impearled—
The ivory model of our future world!'

What though the old and knightly age was o'er!
    Still lived the spirit of true manliness;
Still Beauty guerdoned Courage, as of yore,
    And Courage died for Beauty in distress . . . .
Perplexed at first, Claude was not long delayed—
Here was a woman who had need of aid!

As loyal as the virtuous Bethlamite,
    Who spread his skirt adown the tap'ring limbs
Of the sweet daughter of the Moabite,
    To veil her beauty from the rash moonbeams,
Which slanting cross the lintel, through the door
Beat in a shower on the threshing-floor;

So Claude, without one thought too large that could
   Have shamed ascetic hermitage of yore,
Spread over her but half-masked maidenhood
   The gray capote, or fisher's cloak, he wore,
And shielding thus, he raised her drooping head,
And spanned her wrists to find if she were dead.

The current of her life beat slow and light—
   Her breathing bore its balm as does a spray
Of spicewood in the still Sumatrian night,
   Or Spanish-palms in slumb'rous Balize day:
'Agnes!' said Claude, 'it must be she is thine,
And I will bear her back unto thy shrine.

'Dear lily! whate'er wind hath blown thee here,
   From out yon vestal garden of the Saints—
If evil thought, mad hope, or mishap mere—
   It is my duty to restore thee hence:
I fear thy life hangs in the scale, sweet flower;
Madonna shield thee with protecting power!

'What if it were—but no! it cannot be!' . . . .
   He dared not dwell upon that thought—and yet—
(Or does he dream?) he sees, or fears to see,
   In features cypressed by those locks dew-wet,
A dread similitude—enough to start
The virgin blood to boiling round his heart.

Onward he bore his burden with a tread
    Uneven, for scarce had he time to trace,
In his dear prize, the mould, the hair, the head,
    The faultless features, and the tender grace
Of her with whom his fancy gilded o'er
The world of sight—whose name re-echoed every shore.

Before the shadow of the Convent cast
    Its sombre wings upon his hurried route,
And fearing lest each sigh should be her last,
    He did not dare to pause and solve his doubt,
But trembling with the thought, but half repressed,
He drew his charge more tightly to his breast.

And as the dark old graystone pile he neared,
    Which rose in strength superior to decay,
No sound to match his tread, or drown, he heard,
    Except a lonely watch-dog's deep-mouthed bay;
No porter's challenge met him at the gate,
Nor bar, nor bolt, bade him impatient wait.

Ajar the massive door, upon his touch,
    Upon the poisèd hinge, fell slowly back:
All things within the vestibule were such
    As gave out nakedly a dampness black
And gaunt with mouldy gloom—a cavern, this,
Replete with angels consecrate to peace!

Claude pressed—more tightly pressed—the tender form,
   Which like a sweet love-poem lay within
The parchment-roll of his entwining arm:
   As from the closing of a long ravine,
The mountain cotter's taper gleams by night,
So through the corridor a single light

Romantically lit the passage-term;
   And through the door whence issued this, Claude
      went—
Without a premonition, spread alarm
   Wild through the wimpling veils of nun and saint!
No bell of diver, seeking pearls, could spread
Confusion to the Ocean's heart more dread!

And here were pearls! sweet, precious, garnered pearls,
   Richer than Persian, or Brazilian gem!
Rare stones of Christ, snatched from the eddying whirls
   Of life, to glitter in His diadem!
And here were pearls mured in an ocean cave,
Sparkling 'mid death, like diamonds in a grave!

But Claude, a diver, brought not one away,
   But bore one back, kissed by the waves, mayhap
Too roughly kissed, or flirted by the spray
   Against a rude ledge in the water's lap:
No step profane for years these depths had known—
Claude recked it not, but laid his jewel down!

Now, would that men were not more pure than God!
    And would no ermine whiter were than Heaven!
No paths more straight than those which Jesus trod—
    No laws but those which He Himself hath given!
There were then fewer saints, but more good men—
The hermits rarer, but more Christians then!

Above the ages—through their weird discord—
    We vaguely hear—our hearts grow still to list
The shrieks of fair young maids, with the keen cord
    Cleaving the soft, warm flesh of virgin wrist,
Of perfect arm, down to the ivory bone,
Or with smooth joints dissevered one by one!

And mitred priests, with keys about the belt,
    And childless females beautifully pale,
Who long had lost their names, nor ever felt,
    Or would deny that they did ever feel,
One touch of love to demonstrate them human—
One weakness that had served to prove them woman!

Cold, passionless, to pity merely dead
    For others, or themselves, th' unsparing Three
To whom Hellenic Myth assigned the thread
    Of life, were never more compassion-free,
Than were the judges in these Gothic years,
Who tried the crimes of Faith, or Love, or Tears!

ST. AGNES OF GUIENNE.   149

(This was the deep Red Sea through which we crost
   To reach the wilderness, our present shore :
The Jordan lies beyond, whose milky coast,
   And brazen mountains, filled with precious ore,
Shall make us all forget the erring past,
And symbols know for only such at last!)

And such (save one) the Council called to sit
   In censure, and assign to penance dure,
Hermine, because she had not found it meet
   To perish ere she reached the inlet-shore,
From whose rude sand, which knew not half her worth,
A manly arm redeemed, and bore her forth.

The tale she told was simply told and true—
   It was a ballad which, but drifting on
Poetic souls, had fallen as the dew
   On flowers, soothingly from out the moon,
To touch and woo the sense of pity, till
Sweet balm of fragrant mercy should distill.

Hermine confessed that from the steps of stone,
   Which to the Bath of Saints let down their flight,
Upon the yestreen eve she went alone
   To bathe, as was permitted her that night:
That tempted, by caressing waves, too far,
She ventured almost o'er the Inlet's bar.

Meanwhile the tide arose: the sea, in wroth,
  (And that she had not thought of it before),
Broke on the rocks, a pyramid of froth,
  That blinding, pushed her outward from the shore,
And only Jesu's tender-guiding hand
Enabled her, worn out, to reach the strand.

Now faint from battling the waves, exhaust,
  She scarce could tell what next to her befell;
She must have fallen fainting on the coast;
  By whom relieved (save dreams) she could not tell,
'But God,' she sobbed, 'do so to me, and more,
If act or thought were ever less impure!'

The Abbess rose, an Aquilonian star
  Gilding the sky of judgment, through hoar frost!
'It were not strange,' she said, 'that one so fair
  Should challenge your slight censure at the most,
If she but swam beyond the Bath of Saints,
Led by the curling ripple's blandishments.

'But reverend Bishop, Fathers, Prioress,
  (Such was the Court), the mind conceiving sin
Knows well to paint, with seeming guilelessness,
  In outward fairness what is foul within:
What think ye, Judges, when from me hear,
Within her own correction if I err,

'That he who bore her hither from the coast,
   (By accident, as she pretends, good sooth!)
Nude and submissive in his arms of lust,
   None other was than that rash Guienne youth,
Whose shame, with hers, beneath her father's roof,
Drove Hermine hither, with his stern reproof!'

(With brows of darker censure knit, they now
   Frown on Hermine, quite paralyzed and awk—
A quail pretending death in the windrow,
   Beneath the talons of the sousing hawk—)
'Shall I pronounce your sentence with one breath?
Her vow is broke! the penalty is Death!'

The Guienne maid is sweet, nor born for strife—
   A fragrance from an aromatic vale—
In Sabbaths of the year, a thing of life,
   But perishing in storm and wintry gale—
A thing of much dear promise, if not killed
By some keen frost of wrong too early chilled.

Struck by the Abbess' clear, transfixing eyes—
   Serenely beautiful, but pitiless,
As stars that shine in hyperboreal skies,
   Beyond the bourn of ultrakanic seas—
Poor Hermine gave one look as all were o'er,
Then fainting, prostrate sank upon the floor.

One priest, quite young, more troubled than the rest,
  Sprang up as if to catch the falling flower,
But checked himself, as though the thought confessed,
  Would wrong his office, or offend some power:
The Abbess rang a bell that near her lay—
The Nun that answered bore Hermine away.

The noblest things forever are most rare!
  A woman just! An Englishman polite!
A maiden without vanity, though fair!
  A Frenchman wedded less to form than right!
A priest with less of zeal than sanctitude!
A wise man modest, or a great one good!

The Bishop still sat reading in his chair:
  The golden cross fell on the table nigh;
Above a cloud of finest snow-white hair,
  The crimson mitre crowned his forehead high:
His open cassock left to view the milk
Of his white surplice of Sicilian silk:

While that Hermine confessed he read straight on;
  When th' Abbess had begun he turned a leaf,
Nor raised his head until her speech was done,
  Her judgment rendered with its weight of grief:
When Hermine fell, he simply held his peace,
His book on end, his finger in his place.

When, as the morning bears a pallid mist,
    The sister bore Hermine away, he rose:
The tassel of his cassock 'bout his waist,
    Catching his chair, he paused to set it loose:
As starlight gilding a cathedral aisle,
Cromal, rich-stained, so broke his wondrous smile.

Upon his features, seemingly, their sate
    Mysterious dreams of melancholy faith;
Their beauty soft, but not effeminate—
    Such as the picture of Augustin hath:
His brows branched upward from his Grecian nose,
As a straight oak his first two branches throws.

A far-off flame, from out the mystic East,
    Lit up his eyes—an apostolic gaze,
And legendary look, that marked him priest,
    In mute significance upon a face
That knew more than the simple laymen should,
Yet sought to use it only for their good.

His head was rounder than the solid earth—
    A planet circling 'bout the Church of Rome,
The sun where all his ideas had their birth,
    And every aspiration had its home;
His faith the radius-vector of his mind,
Which bound its circle, and his hopes defined.

And as he rose, he robbed the angry Sun
    Of holy kisses, where his shadow fell
Upon a picture on the wainscot, drawn
    In freshness worthy of Herrara's skill,
Depicting Agnes, as she lay in dream,
Soft-threading which, the Snowy Mother came.

A robe of leopard skins thrown o'er her form,
    Disposed in tumbled luxury, left bare
Her throat, and just a hint of bust; one arm
    Lapped o'er the tide of wavy, raven hair;
The other at the elbow bent, and prest,
Emergent from the robe, upon her breast.

Thus slept—immaculately slept—the Saint;
    The Virgin hovered o'er her, clothed upon
With sunlight, crowned with a full complement
    Of glorious stars; beneath her curved the moon;
On either side, cherubic pinions beat
Upon the lucent air about her feet.

The Prelate's voice had some strange power to please,
    Like a most friendly greeting in the dark,
Or carriage-wheels through arching cedar trees
    At bottom of an old, majestic park,
Which make the gardener pause from work to hear,
Bent o'er his spade, his foot uplift in air.

'My friends,' he said, 'far be from me to seem
    Indifferent to crime, or false to truth ;
To punish one, reflect the other's beam,
    Transmitted us from God's perpetual youth,
As light to star from central-burning Sun,
Is our commission—a most sacred one !

'Nor deem that I ignore the latitude
    Vice gives itself in this distempered age ;
How, scorning law, and every sanctitude,
    From thrones to hovels, lust and passion rage—
From Lent to Carnival corruption reigns,
And barters souls within our very fanes.

'And yet, as that Apostle whom Christ loved
    Could preach but Love, and only that thenceforth,
So we, whom our superior passion moved,
    Forsaking paltry elements of earth,
To lie on Jesu's breast, should, from His touch,
Learn only Mercy renders Justice such !

' 'Tis not the young—believe me, it is not
    Young golden-headed girls of Christ, whose sin
Leaves on our Church's ermine foulest blot—
    'Tis not poor blue-eyed virgins, like Hermine,
Whose errors stain the solar robe of her
Who wears the stars through God's eternal year !

' 'Tis that the hand, which, holding Justice' scales,
    Should be as equal as eternal truth,
Relaxes grasp to clutch at gold, and sells
    To wealth what it denies to honest ruth:
'Tis that the base to high positions rise,
And ravished Law on her own altars dies!

' I would not grant indulgence to the king,
    To father contemplated wrong or sin;
I would not shrive an emperor a thing
    Which he did not repent, or still persisted in:
But ah! when weakness pleads for mercy, I
Were shaming Christ, to bid the contrite die!

' And a mere accident! the act of God,
    Which we pronounce, for our convenience, Chance,
(Which is but law less known and understood,)
    Brings crime alone to gross improvidence:—
Who will affirm, that by design prepence,
This Novice swam beyond the Bath of Saints?

' Can it be thought there was concerted plan
    Of sinful trysting at the Inlet-side,
Between her and this native of Guienne?
    Abbess! if so, what liberty too wide
Is this allowed the nurslings in your charge,
That they communicate with men at large?

'If not by chance they met, but by design,
　　Who can believe he would return her 'neath
This Convent-roof, consenting to resign
　　Himself to danger, and his love to death?
Not so! In everything I see confirmed
The accident the child herself affirmed.

'I see in her misfortune, but no crime—
　　For sin, I see a miracle unfold
To us the sov'reign will, through grace sublime,
　　Of Him who rules by wonders, as of old!
To these young shipwrecks on the coast of woe,
Methinks God points the path which they should go.

'But fearing lest I should, in evil hour,
　　Construing Providence, presume too far,
And having witnessed oft displays of power
　　Miraculous, by Her we worship here,
I'll pray our Mother and Her Saint make plain
The guilt or innocence of this young twain.

'In that flush age when the great Tuscan drew,
　　And Da Vinci breathèd beauty into stone,
A Spanish sculptor, dying young, and who
　　Is known to fame by this success alone,
Unfolded, from his years of labor spent,
In white Carrara marble carved, our Saint.

ST. AGNES OF GUIENNE.

' Not few the miracles She has performed ;
   And I myself bear witness that Her smile,
Once when some glorious diapason warmed
   The palpitating air, broke forth the while ;
And once at Mass, when levity was shown,
Methought I heard the Marble Maiden groan.

' The purest things this earth has ever known—
   The violet's involute—fresh dew—new wine—
Are not so pure as this quick-breathing stone,
   Rounded in mould of chastity divine ;
Informed with old serenity, debased
By no lewd hintings of the modern taste.

' I feel if this design, so sacred-white,
   Were brought in contact with somewhat profane,
Saint Agnes, from her own celestial height,
   Would whirl in living currents her disdain,
Until they broke the frozen bonds of stone,
And wrinkled all her beauty in a frown.

' If, on the other part, my voice invoke
   Her aid to render innocence more plain,
She who herself to answered prayer awoke
   From dreams of love betrayed and sequent pain,
Will by some token vindicate the name
Of sweet virginity, and maiden fame.

'Before you, Judges, and before the Saints,
    And Sisters of this Abbey of the Snow,
In yonder Chapel, an half hour hence,
    Saint Agnes, by some miracle, may throw
Her own sunlight upon the clouds which wear
The hue of guilt above this youthful pair.'

The Bishop thus: anon the Chapel call
    Once, twice and thrice gave out its clear-toned voice,
And chamber doors were heard to turn, and all
    The Abbey bustle with unusual noise;
The school for Novices came to a close,
And 'mong these angels chirping wonder rose.

Drifting like dogwood blossoms in the Spring,
    Or white peonies in a wind of May,
Through the long corridor's rear opening,
    Which led into the Court, across which lay
The solid Chapel steps of smooth-worn stones,
Glided the cream-dressed novices and nuns.

The Gothic Chapel of the Snow was low,
    But full of legendary ornament;
The outside rough, the inside rich with show,
    Like the mean casing of a glorious saint;
Endowed by legacies, her temple shone
Through generations, from fair Agnes down.

Colossal forms around the pillared throne;
    Mosaic groups of crucificial mould;
Vines arabesque, and mystic roses strewn
    O'er fields of blue, with stars of burning gold;
Glories surrounding heads with jewels crowned;
The ceiling thick with wings, with saints the ground.

Saints Genevieve, Cecelia, Magdalene;
    The hierarchal choirs of heaven above;
Far-flashing girdles; fountains crystaline;
    Virgins beneath the rainbow-tinted dove . . . .
Each symbol with which Faith inflamed the heart
Here Genius married to eternal art!

Cent'ring a cirque of most celestial forms,
    There stood, a type of all that ransoms men,
Chaste as the glist of her petrific charms,
    The statue of Saint Agnes of Guienne:
Filled with divinest sorrow, her cold eyes
Turned up their frozen lashes to the skies.

Just where her tunic cleft the twin-orbed hills,
    Whose sweet Carrara firmness swelled below,
A rose-bud opened out its carvèd frills,
    In foliations of most spotless snow;
Its cup indented showed upon its spars
The very furze, hair-fine, the calix bears.

ST. AGNES OF GUIENNE.

From out the core a wingèd insect peered,
  So finely wrought the tentacles were seen—
The feet, the shell, the very eyes appeared,
  And the small claws and horns for ravage keen;
Already subtile fringes beveled out,
Showed where his depredating saws had cut.

The saintly feet were bare; beneath one heel
  A miniature was pressed, without disdain,
And yet with passion's energy, until
  The perfect toes were raised up from the plane:
The whole expression was divine, and meant
  A woman crucified to form a saint.

When all were seat, their genuflexions o'er,
  The Bishop came with slow and reverend pace;
His manner meek, his eyes upon the floor,
  Till in the Council's midst he took his place;
With folded arms there stood near by, o'erawed,
  But brave in conscience still, Hermine and Claude.

He loosely clad in Guienne fisher's dress—
  A short-sleeved jacket of the jauntiest green;
Superbly pallid unto ghostliness,
  More white than her white frock, appeared Hermine,
Whose manner, radiant with girlish grace,
In every Judge's heart (save one) made place.

The Abbess, like a type of beauty wrought
   In sculptured marble, sat unmoved through all;
An intellect pure crystal—frozen thought—
   A saint, if such can be, without a soul—
A woman, born of one, if such can be,
Without one spark of human sympathy.

'Through the confessional,' the prelate said,
   'The law forbids me telling when or where,
Two robes have I obtained; this one, and made
   Deftly, was brought to me since past a year;
The other is the gray capote Claude wore,
And with it swathed this child upon the shore:

'The first let laymen—angels—name!
   'Tis white as snow yet undivorced from air;
But, if it should prove black with maiden blame,
   Its stain is darker than its texture fair;
Nor shall we lack a mistress for its sin,
Since on the marge her name I find, 'Hermine!'

'Upon our saintly Founder's effigy,
   Mould in Carrara marble, white as heaven,
By some great artist o'er the Spanish sea,
   And thence to fame and to our Convent given,
I now propose these vestures to suspend,
And on her face the issue will depend.

ST. AGNES OF GUIENNE.

' A voice foretells me if these robes are pure,
    Saint Agnes' smile will brighten as the sky;
If otherwise, when stained with sin, they o'er
    Her marble form immaculate shall lie,
Mark me, Saint Agnes' wrath will frown and flush
More conscious than a living maiden's blush!'

Some eyes were there who had not seen for years
    (Save dreams), the face of an unshaven man!
The prospect troubled them, and moved such tears
    As only long-forgotten memories can:
And they were moved, and woman . . nature . . pain . .
Old, darling dreams retouched . . . came back again.

And there was one suspended fragrant breath
    Of sympathy for both (but more for Claude),
What time the test of guilt, for life or death,
    The Court submitted, as it were, to God:
Hermine leaned on her lover, and her eyes
Recked not the scene, but counseled with the skies.

Then o'er the shoulder of the marble thought,
    The Bishop laid the Guienne capote's ply;
O'er this the maiden's night-robe, deftly wrought,
    Which clung to it far down the saintly thigh,
Like mist clings to an old gray-beaten rock—
A spray of fringe-tree on a scaly oak!

At first a twinkle on the forehead gleamed,
    That intermitting, flushed again, and fell
And burned, till all aglow, her features beamed;
    The rose-bud trembled to a gentle swell . . .
The roundly chiseled, wedded lips unsealed,
    In magic circles, and a smile revealed!

A murmured joy gained on th' expectant air;
    All saw the statue smile, or thought they saw;
'A miracle! Praise to Saint Agnes there!'
    They cry, and bow or kneel in rev'rent awe,
The cause itself now for the time passed o'er,
In wonder at the Saint's supernal power.

At length the prelate waving silence : 'Bless,
    Yea, all that is within us, bless His name,
Who grants this office to our Patroness
    To shelter innocence from unjust shame!
His be the glory, ours, through grace, the power
To read the proper lesson from the hour.

'This Novice is not yet a bride of Christ,
    Nor could be such till that supremest hour,
Which by the last most solemn Eucharist
    Makes her a queen who was but maid before—
With bridal veil of black exchanged for white,
Makes her a Nun who was but Neophyte.

'Nor is it every Novice should be Nun;
   It is a solemn and majestic thing,
This nuptial with the ever-peerless Son!
   And woe if we unwilling brides shall bring
Unto His shrine, who calls His service free—
The highest, only perfect liberty!

'Now 'tis not strange beneath this Hermine's zone
   Should beat a heart rebellious to such thralls;
Her rosy teens have scarcely bloomed full-blown—
   Her fancy wings its flight from out these walls,
And flutt'ring through her veil, bears back her soul
To scenes not long walked through in girlish role.

'All maids are not for Nuns, nor men for Priests,
   Else were our world unpeopled by its creed!
The Father writes our missions in our breasts,
   Which fix our callings, if we give them heed;
Methinks by signs, which we call accidents,
God marks this twain for lovers, not for saints.

'By His authority, and in His name,
   I, His interpreter, within my sphere,
These twain affianced man and wife proclaim,
   And by due service will unite them here,
The smiles of saints, apostles, angels under—
Whom God hath joined let not man put asunder!'

Then o'er them, like a spotless mantle, fell
    The marriage-service of the Church of Rome.
The fair young Neophyte, from lily-pale
    To crimson, felt the color go and come,
As if a pure white butterfly, with wing
Translucent, crept athwart a rose of Spring.

The Convent Vespers trembled toward the Sea;
    And Incarnation, and Eternal Bliss,
And Resurrection, and Virginity,
    And Intercession—Passion—Christian Peace—
All Sacred Mysteries, poured in one stream
Of twilight service, closing with this Hymn:

        Nivalis in candore,
        Bright through eternity,
        Star of the hoary Sea,
            Ave!
        We, in humility,
        Bow to thy majesty,
        Star of our destiny,
            Ave!

        Lo! in her dire distress,
        Thou, in thy tenderness,
        Cam'st to our Patroness—
            Ave!

Thou too hast suffered grief,
Thou too hast found relief—
O! make our sorrows brief!
    Ave!

Mother of Mystery!
Intacta Virgo! We
Ring out thy jubilee—
    Ave!
Hark to thy Chapel bell,
Anthem on anthem swell!
Audi nos! Guard us well!
    Ave!

Agnes conjuring thee,
Hear us imploring thee,
Salvis a te adhunc,
Cara Nivalis, tunc,
Ora pro nobis nunc—
Ave Maria, Mother of Snow!

Then went Hermine to say her sweet good-byes,
  Delighted at the cause, yet sad to part;
With a most heavenly pity in her eyes,
  And a delicious hunger at her heart;
A virgin fragrance lifting its sweet spell
From out the cincture of a cloistered dell!

Soft Twilight fills the world with harmony;
    The measuring Sun has scored the level day;
The silver-sandaled Tide-Queen audibly
    Calls to the pulses of the ebbing Bay;
The ruby Evening-Star, a stemless rose,
Bossed on the shield of Night, in Heaven glows.

From many a darkling chink, despite their vows,
    The angel eyes of Nuns fling moistened light,
Like fire-flies sparkling through the drooping boughs
    Of weeping willows, in the Southern night,
Or starry clusters, when but few are left
Unhid by clouds, through some fantastic rift.

The twain pass on in unrestricted joy,
    Whole atmospheres above a careful world!
Their dew-bathed brows seem touching on the sky,
    And clouds beneath their footsteps are unfurled;
Their arms clasp benedictions, and embrace
Eternity—though homeless, theirs all space.

Beside their path a blooming orange stands;
    In center lies, from the conservatoir,
A melon, broken in the pathway's sands,
    Full ripe, with crisp, green rind, and crimson core;
Upon the left, clematis, from a bole
Of fig, blows whitely as the bridal soul.

'Great God!' the good man cries, 'how we do mar
  The grand proportions of our glorious creed!
In vain hast Thou created all things fair,
  And showered far more bounties than we need!
We set our will Thy steadfast laws above,
  Ignore the heart, and beat down youthful love!

'Great Solitude! whose throne is in yon sea
  Of crystal, and beneath whose feet are pent
Exhaustless sources of immensity,
  Eternal, and above the firmament—
How long! how long! ye Nightwinds, with your song!
Ye Waves! Sweet Stars! O, answer me, how long!'

Then with his eyes, across the winding hill,
  As through the dusk their youthful figures glide,
The good man, murmuring benedictions still,
  Pursues the husband and his virgin bride;
But as he turns to make the postern fast,
Lo! three young swallows fly from a sweet nest!